£3·99

Christn

④/16

Dearest Simon

Wis

I th

prep

G000116293

# Dallaglio
# on Rugby

# Dallaglio on Rugby

## Know the Modern Game

### Lawrence Dallaglio
### with Chris Jones

Hodder & Stoughton

First published in Great Britain in 1998
by Hodder and Stoughton
A division of Hodder Headline PLC

British Library Cataloguing in Publication Data

ISBN: 0 340 71839 0

Design/make up by Roger Walker

Printed and bound in Great Britain by
Butler & Tanner Ltd, Frome and London

Hodder and Stoughton
A division of Hodder Headline PLC
338 Euston Road
London NW1 3BH

# Contents

*To Alice, Ella, my sister Francesca and my parents,*
*Vincent and Eileen, with love*

# Acknowledgements

I would like to express my sincere thanks to Chris Jones for all his hard work in helping me to produce this book. A big hand to Ashley Woolfe for always managing to stay one step ahead of me at all times. Thank you to the photographers, AllSport, Colorsport and 'PA' News, who have contributed their work, and a special word to Roddy Bloomfield, my publisher, for his infectious enthusiasm and eagerness, not to mention his patience, right up to the final whistle.

# Introduction

Rugby is undergoing phenomenal change and it is impacting on players, administrators and the many thousands who come through the turnstiles. We have all been touched in some way by the move to professionalism and, even though you may not be paid and are happy to play at your own level, there is a knock-on effect. The infighting amongst the game's rulers in England has ensured that the debate over who actually controls the sport has been back-page news for nearly two years. The players have been caught in the middle and it's been a testing time for everyone involved in the sport. This book is an attempt to give the reader an insight into the demands of the modern game and what it means to those who play at the very highest level.

Instead of leading England on their 1998 summer tour to New Zealand, Australia and South Africa, I was forced to stay at home by a shoulder injury which flared up during a long and demanding mixture of international, European and domestic rugby. I am passionate about my rugby and the fact that I had to miss an international tour was a devastating blow. To measure yourself as a player, you have to take on the best and meeting the All Blacks, Wallabies and Springboks in a five-week period was a challenge I would have relished.

The Southern Hemisphere is the power base of the game and we can only raise our own standards by taking on the three great nations who have all won the World Cup. We toured without eighteen front-line players and suffered a series of big defeats. That was hard for me to take because, as captain, I wanted to be there, standing alongside the others wearing the red rose.

I was given the choice of touring and possibly putting myself in a position where an operation was needed, or of standing down and letting time and treatment heal the problem. With the World Cup on the horizon, I had no option but to take care of my body and ensure that I would be fit and raring to go at the start of what should be a momentous season. I was not pressurised by my club, Wasps, to miss the tour. It was a decision I took after seeking the advice of people who know what they are talking about. In the end it came down to me and I stand by that decision.

Top class rugby, as this book attempts to explain, has become a hugely demanding professional sport. All those who play have to adopt a professional attitude because the game is no longer a pastime – it is a job. Livelihoods are on the line and you would be mad to put yourself in a position where injury could leave you on the scrap heap. I am contracted to my club and I also have an England contract and there are certain criteria that must be satisfied. I have to look after my body because the club, quite rightly, considers its players to be assets. This is a fact of professional rugby life and one all of us are going to have to come to terms with.

It is vital that everyone involved in the English game pulls in the same direction and the ultimate goal must be to produce the strongest possible England team. If the national team is successful then the clubs will reap a massive benefit. The World Cup is that tantalising goal and nothing should be allowed to deflect our attention from that target. I have spent the summer getting myself into the right shape and level of fitness to play my part and I cannot wait for the season to start.

I hope this book helps you to gain even more enjoyment from the game and an understanding of what it takes to get fifteen guys on to the pitch every Saturday.

# 1
# Why I love rugby union

I remember arriving at Ampleforth School clutching my beloved football, still intent on forging a career as a professional player. Although barely in my teens, I was going to be the next George Best or Peter Osgood. As I looked out on to the playing fields of that famous Catholic school, I counted twenty-seven sets of rugby posts and not one pitch marked out for football. It suddenly dawned on me that my sporting life was about to undergo a radical change and that round ball was quickly hidden away from prying eyes.

Ampleforth believed in rugby union with a passion I had not encountered before. I come from an Italian background where football is the major sport and this is true for England, too. All my early days had been spent kicking a football around whenever I got the chance to play with my friends, and Mum was forever washing kit and muddied school clothes. My parents chose Ampleforth because they wished me to enjoy the best possible Catholic education. Sport did not come into their equation, although football came into mine until I saw that forest of uprights and discovered that there was more than one religion at Ampleforth.

I wasn't a virgin when it came to rugby union because my friend Franksie had taken me along to Staines RFC to sample mini-rugby and I had enjoyed the experience. I didn't understand the laws (and some would say I still don't!) and those early games seemed to involve me kicking the ball whenever it came my way. The other boys were intent on getting hold of the ball, running for as long as they could in no particular direction and then giving it to someone else when they had done enough and needed a rest. It was obvious that rugby was for people who were trying to express themselves in a variety of ways, even the poor six-year-old who was expected to kick a conversion over posts set up for adults!

I was fascinated by the whole experience but the game did not usurp football in my heart until many years later when Ampleforth had given me the chance to win selection for representative sides. By then I had discovered that rugby union offers something for everyone and I don't say that as some kind of

My first international try for England against Western Samoa in December 1995.

glib comment. This is a sport that consumes me with a passion and it's only natural for me to want it to be even more successful.

I was drawn to the game because I wanted to take part, but there are many millions around the world who love to watch rugby, never having played the game. They become hooked because they see its showcase games on television. This book is for players who want to get to the top of their game, but it is for the onlookers, too, so that they can understand the stresses and the calculations of the modern game at the highest level.

At this level today the sport has gone professional and there is a danger that a yawning chasm will exist between the pro and amateur games. We all

play the same sport, it's just that part of rugby has evolved into a professional section. I see no reason why the two cannot continue to live under the same roof. We should be stronger because of our expansion, not weaker. Convincing more people to play and watch rugby is vital and a task that should be undertaken by everyone involved in the game from mini-rugby right up to international level. Look at women's rugby – a real growth area in England, and the women won the World Cup which is something the men's national team has yet to manage!

## What is rugby union?

Well, for a start it is not called rugger. I play rugby and the union version rather than the league game which is native to the North of England and started when broken-time payments were requested by players. How times change! I never refer to my chosen sport as rugger because that is a public-school term which rhymes with something else and harks back to a past life. The game, as we all know, was invented at Rugby School, not somewhere called Rugger, when William Webb Ellis first picked up the ball illegally and ran with it in 1823. From that moment millions of youngsters around the world have, like myself, grown to love the game that Webb Ellis is credited with creating. And, like him, we have all followed suit, breaking the rules of the game and getting penalised for our efforts! Webb Ellis's innovation of running with the ball was regarded as of doubtful legality for some time. It was the norm to catch the ball during a game at Rugby School and then have the opportunity to kick it forward. Some people (mainly from our Celtic cousin countries) claim that many English teams still do that! Try-scoring evolved from the fact that a team earned 'the right to try for goal' after they touched the ball down over the opposition line. It wasn't until the start of the 1970s that the try became worth more than a penalty goal and this was a legacy of those early days when the kick between the uprights was the main objective. Today the game is doing its best to increase the opportunity to score tries because fans love to see the ball being touched down. Kicking still has an important role to play in the game but we all want to see tries and the law-makers have recognised this fact.

As players we are all desperate to experience the exhilaration of scoring a try. You never get tired of putting that ball down on or over the opposition line. It doesn't matter if your team is being badly beaten, the sheer delight of having made it to the line is worth battling for under any circumstances. My first international try came against Western Samoa and I can still remember the elation that coursed through my body. It was the ultimate rugby high and you become addicted to the drug. A warning note – perhaps that's why so many try-scoring chances are lost through self-interest. We all want to take the ball over the line and normal judgement can go out of the window.

# 2

# The positions

## Full back

It's a position that requires myriad skills and the man wearing No. 15 has to be a footballer, in the broadest sense. He is also the last line of defence because he is the man who is often faced with a one-on-one tackle, aware that a mistake will cost the team dearly.

Although it is now seen as a negative response to kick possession back at the opposition, unless of course it is into space, the full back must have a sound kicking game to fall back on when running the ball out of defence is not a viable option. He can also be the team's main goal-kicker as this takes away one of the extra responsibilities from an outside half.

In defence, the full back must be confident in his ability to catch the up-and-under kicks from the opposition. This is still a prime way of causing mayhem near the posts, and with a mark now able to be claimed with your feet off the ground, the full back can halt an attack dead with his ability to jump and catch the high kick.

His tackling has to be sound and supported by pace because on many occasions the full back will be moving across to make a cover tackle against an opponent who is already travelling at top speed. Timing the tackle and being prepared for any change of direction come with experience and the best full backs try and outpsyche their opponents before the tackle is made.

In attack, the full back is one of the most potent weapons any team can possess because he can join the three-quarter line at pace to create the all important extra man. Defences these days are excellent at shuffling across the pitch to deny the opposition space so attacking options which offer the full back the opportunity to become a surprise strike force are crucial.

Christian Cullen of New Zealand possesses all of the above skills and is rightly considered amongst the best No. 15s in the game at present. His try-scoring record shows how crucial a full back with real pace can be.

# Right and left wing

Although there are many players who can play in either wing position, they do require particular skills. The wing is normally the quickest player in the team and the aim is to get him into space and let that speed do the rest. However, the days when you could afford to carry a fast man who did not have other skills are over.

The wings have to play a major role in defensive patterns these days and form a critical 'back three' with the full back. When a high kick is launched at the full back, the wings have to ensure they are in support of the ball-catcher either to set up a maul or launch a counter-attack which utilises their latent pace.

Right wings should cultivate an ability to side-step off their right foot, which brings them infield and back towards their support runners. This move,

*Left:* New Zealand's Christian Cullen, the ultimate strike full back.

*Right:* Ieuan Evans comes off his right foot to outfox the defence.

*Below:* Will Carling sets Jerry Guscott free in attack.

used in conjunction with the outside swerve, is aimed at putting doubt into the cover defence and the full back in particular. Ieuan Evans of Wales is a great exponent of the side-step and outside swerve and his try record proves this.

Left wings prefer to come off their left foot and then look for space or support and also have that option of going on the outside. Of course, there are always exceptions and Jonah Lomu, the New Zealand giant, has the strength and power to run right through a would-be tackler without needing to avoid contact.

# Inside and outside centres

Centres, like wings, often prefer to specialise. Will Carling and Jerry Guscott, England's record-breaking centres, adopted the inside (Carling) and outside (Guscott) roles throughout their careers. The inside centre attempts to interest the opposition by straightening the attack to stop the defenders from just drifting across the field and cutting down the space available for the wing. The outside centre is aiming to exploit the hesitancy in the defence that his centre partner has created by running at the opposition. While a player like Carling had pace, it was his strength to absorb the tackle and then pass the ball to Guscott that often created space for his colleague. Guscott's outstanding pace would then take him in behind the defensive line and that allowed his full back and wing to offer support to carry on the raid.

Defensive patterns revolve around the centre pairing and the Carling/Guscott duo were renowned for shoring up the England midfield with their ability to shuffle across the pitch and use their pace to snuff out any half-breaks. Verbal communication between the centres is absolutely essential and experience brings with it an ability to read what the opposition is going to try and pull off in attack. A strong midfield defence can reduce the opposition to relying on the kick to get them up field.

# Outside half

The No. 10 is the critical position in any back division. He becomes the focal point in attack and defence and is the man given responsibility for calling the moves and options. Nothing happens by chance these days and every No. 10 has, in his head, a large number of options to suit each and every situation. He is constantly talking to his scrum half, centres and open side flanker who will have to be in support of whichever back move he calls.

He is often the goal-kicker and is expected to possess a wide range of kicking talents out of the hand to supplement the running game he initiates. It is the position that attracts the most praise but also the most criticism.

Michael Lynagh of Australia holds the world record for points scored in test matches and also masterminded his country's 1991 World Cup triumph. Lynagh with the combination of his defensive tackling and attacking breaks to open up defences was a player of outstanding all-round footballing ability and a model for the No. 10 role.

# Scrum half

This is the vital link position between the backs and forwards. If the scrum half is under pressure, the whole team will suffer. He must be a livewire player, someone who is always talking to his No. 10 and his forwards. Communication is crucial for this position and he is never out of the action. Passing has to be quick and reliable off both right and left hands and his kicking game is equally important. With space for the backs at a premium, the scrum half has to be quick and strong enough to look for holes around the set pieces and rucks and mauls.

Kyran Bracken of England is considered by many to be the ideal size for a scrum half, possessing speed, strength, passing and kicking skills to bring the best out of himself and those around him. These guys need to be durable because they take a lot of punishment. Opponents know that if you can hamper the scrum half your chances of success are greatly increased. The scrum half also has a vital role to play in defence where he can often be the final tackler as he covers behind the backs.

# Loose head prop

The world of the front-row forwards is a dark and murky one and the loose head is one of the strong men of the game. He has to ensure his hooker has the best possible chance of striking for the ball at the put-in at the scrum. The opposition prop will be dipping his shoulder to try and obscure the ball from the hooker's view, while the loose head attempts to keep him up. It's all-in wrestling with seven other players in your scrum trying their best to help out in whatever way they can. On the opposition ball, the loose head attempts to drive the opposition tight head up and backwards to disrupt and upset planned moves.

Besides this scrum role, the loose head prop must lift his jumpers at the line out, secure the ball once it has been won at the line out and clear out opponents at rucks and mauls. Props are also expected to be in support of the ball around the pitch, making it a demanding all-round job. Scotland's Tom Smith was the ideal loose head prop on the Lions tour and showed all these skills.

Michael Lynagh gets to grips with me!

Kyran Bracken – an ideal size for a No. 9 and not intimidated by Jason Leonard.

The Destroyer – Jeff Probyn causes mayhem for the opposition.

# Hooker

This is a position for the masochist. You spend your scrums hanging between two props while the opposition attempt to get their heads, arms and any other parts of their bodies in your face. The hooker's prime responsibility is to secure the ball from the set pieces. This means striking for the ball at the scrums and throwing in accurately to the jumpers at the line out. The scrum strike is not a simple swing of the leg, as there are various channels by which the ball can travel back to the No. 8. It depends on the hooker's skill to get the ball into the right channel to allow the chosen move to be called.

The line out is often more important than the scrum and getting the ball to your jumpers should be simpler now that lifting is legal. The best hookers are as good as darts professionals – able to hit double top every time. However, bad weather can turn this task into a real lottery and calls for even more skill and accuracy. Besides winning all of this ball, the hooker is expected to act as an extra back-row forward in the loose and most importantly to have the ability to read the game. Sean Fitzpatrick has become the best hooker in the world because he possesses all the above skills.

# Tight head prop

This man is the cornerstone of the scrum. If your tight head prop is under pressure then the whole scrum is in difficulty. His main task is to pack down in such a way as to be able to take all the pressure the opposition try to put on him. The tight head needs strong legs to take the scrum low and hold it there with so much pressure coming through his body. On the opposition ball, the tight head is aiming to be a major irritation, one who causes his opposition all kinds of uncomfortable hassles. Jeff Probyn of England was renowned for getting his opposite number upset. Probyn would take the scrum very low, courtesy of his great leg strength, and then angle in to put his head right up against the hooker's face. It sounds as unpleasant as it was for the poor opponent.

Besides this taxing work, the tight head must support at the line out, secure ball and then get around the pitch to shore up rucks and mauls, plus make his fair share of tackles in the loose.

# The second row

The tall men of the game in the second row have become real athletes in recent years. It is now no longer good enough just to be 6ft 8ins because second rows must bring mobility and explosive power to loose play, as well as skill and strength to the line out and scrum.

These players are also known as locks and that is exactly the role they have at the scrum. Their power is needed to enable the front row to operate successfully. Feet positions are vital because they must ensure the ball moves swiftly back in the scrum after the hooker has struck for it.

The line out is their domain and lifting should ensure that men like Martin Johnson of England and Ian Jones of New Zealand always win the ball that is thrown their way. An athletic second row is worth his weight in gold and allows a team to build an entire game plan around his ball-winning abilities.

# Blind side flanker

The man in the No. 6 jersey is a player of proven defensive qualities. The blind side flanker has to put in big tackles to shore up his side of the scrum and around the fringes of rucks and mauls. He can also be an extra option at the line out, as well as a lifter of the middle line-out jumper. Good back rows work as real units, with the blind side flanker going about his business in an unfussy manner particularly in the rucks and mauls where he will attempt to win back the ball for his own side. François Pienaar of South Africa is a good example of a blind side flanker who refused to allow the opposition an easy time in any phase of play and put in huge tackles to stifle attacks.

# Open side flanker

He wears the No. 7 jersey and is the link man and support runner who must be first to the break down when his team is attacking. An open side flanker must have good pace and reliable hands, allied to a predatory nature that makes ball-hunting his main delight. The No. 7 has to put pressure on the opposition No. 10 and work in conjunction with his own outside half to supplement attacks. The open side flanker often has the kind of skills associated with the backs but the mentality and strength of a forward. Michael Jones of New Zealand has been an outstanding open side for more than a decade and set the standard for everyone who wants to wear the No. 7 jersey.

# No. 8

This is the position of control at the scrum. The No. 8 has the responsibility of ensuring the move called at the scrum can be initiated by delivering the ball correctly to the scrum half or picking up and driving himself over the gain line. It's a heads-up position in defence because he has to be aware of what the

*Above:* François Pienaar shows his strength in defence.

*Left:* Martin Johnson gets the better of Ian Jones of New Zealand.

opposition is attempting and good defence relies upon good communication with his flankers and the scrum half.

The No. 8 is normally the third most important jumper at the line out and is often used to deflect ball down to a teammate who is on the peel. Someone like Zinzan Brooke of New Zealand epitomises the kind of skills you need to be a top class No. 8. He is a genuine footballer with a great appreciation of his position on the pitch and what type of situation could develop in both attack and defence. The No. 8 can have a massive influence on the game as he is constantly in possession of the ball.

# 3
# Forty minutes each way

## The kick off

The kick off is a sprint for the team chasing the ball, you cannot just jog forward. It's a battle charge when you can make your first major physical statement. This is the other opportunity, besides the tackle, to make a real impression, legally, on the opposition. Every chasing player has a specific role and like a football throw-in from touch, there isn't any offside which can lead to an angry reaction from the crowd.

There are many different ways of using the kick off, but basically you are either trying to win the ball back yourselves or to force the opposition to kick it into touch deep in their own half to give your side a line out. Just make sure that you kick the thing far enough. For a forward, there is nothing more frustrating than psyching yourself up for the kick off, chasing like a guided missile over 10 metres to try and get the ball back, only to discover your kicker has made a real hash of everything and you have to traipse back to the halfway line and scrum down with the opposition having the put-in and the chance to dictate play right from the first minute.

That is why the specialist kicker in each team spends hours practising kick offs and drop-out kicks on halfway. It has become a precise science with different calls for kicks that travel deep into the opposition half and require your wing to chase at top speed, or the kick that just clears the 10 metre line and allows the entire pack to pressurise the opposition as they attempt to catch the ball. It is possible to isolate one player and drop the ball onto him, targeting an area for attack which you reckon gives you the best chance of winning back possession.

If you are receiving the kick off you must retain possession but it is one of the few areas of the game where there is a genuine fifty-fifty chance of getting the ball if it's a good kick. There is nothing more demoralising for a team that has just conceded a score than to have to restart and see the opposition secure the ball and start moving forward again. There are so many different kinds of restart kicks because the drop out allows the ball to hang in the air and that gives the chasers time to arrive.

# The drop out on the 22

This is needed to restart play after an attacking team has failed in its attempt to score a try, kick a penalty goal or drop a goal, and the defending side touches the ball down themselves over their own line, or the ball goes out of play behind the try line. Like the restart kicks on halfway that I have already mentioned, the drop out from the 22 metre line requires skill from the kicker to get it right. Failure can be even more dangerous than a fluffed restart kick. The fact that you have messed up a kick just 22 metres from your line offers the opposition a great attacking position and thoughts about maybe stringing up your kicker start to gather pace! The crowd will be making their opinion unmistakable as well. This you can do without.

# Attacking patterns

You have to test the opposition out by constantly probing areas of potential weakness and your game plan is designed to achieve that end. Maintaining variety is a key element because you must keep the opposition guessing. Varying the options taken and the speed at which you operate are other fundamentals which, when used correctly, can expose individuals and the opposition as a whole.

These attacking patterns are designed to unlock the defence and rely upon players recognising what type of defence the opposition are operating. If the opposition are drifting across, then you will have to try and use ploys that stop their men from moving towards the touchline and cramping the space you need to create for your wing. This can be achieved in various ways, including the full back coming into the three-quarter line as the extra attacker, or by working a scissors move which has one of the attacking team running at an oblique angle to the drifting defence. The aim with all of these options is to fracture the defence and get your men in behind the opposition.

# Lines of running

There's a lot of talk these days about lines of running and these are crucial in any match. If you run straight at a man you make his job easy as a would-be tackler and so the aim is to choose an angle of attack that makes it difficult for him to put in a strong tackle. You may remember the pre-match analysis that pointed out he was left-handed, so there could be a weakness in his tackling on the right-hand side of his body. The idea is to run in the direction which causes the most confusion for the defending team and running straight is only effective if the support runners pick a different angle to carry on the attack.

There is also the opportunity to use decoy runners and switch moves which force the defence to react and can put them on the wrong foot at vital moments which can lead to try-scoring opportunities. Decoy runners throw a useful spanner into the defensive works because the opposition start to question who they are meant to be tackling. You don't have to make the attacking option too complicated because all you are trying to achieve is some space to exploit. You can also cause initial confusion through the kick.

# The kicking game in attack

The best teams in the world kick the ball a lot and it's absurd to believe anything else. All of the Southern Hemisphere teams put boot to ball and do it very well – into space. There is no point booting the ball to an opponent and the aim is to find the open areas of the pitch that can put the opposition under pressure and force them either to run from deep or kick to touch and hand you the throw-in. A kick is only as good as the chase and if you send the ball down field and then stand back and admire the effort, the opposition will punish you and all the momentum that could be generated is lost. An effective chase, involving a line of team-mates moving up as one to force the defenders to take a limited number of options, is something that is seen in every match. A lot of people misunderstand the significance of the kick as an attacking weapon and many times during the game you hear the crowd bemoaning the fact that the kicker did not find touch. In most instances he was not trying to reach touch because that immediately gives the ball to the opposition.

In past years it was felt that the outside half and full back were the only players who would need to be able to kick effectively and everyone else could forget about learning this skill. Now it's important that everyone in the back division has the ability to kick and this is particularly true for wingers because they are having to turn around and retrieve ball kicked by the opposition. They cannot always run this possession back out of defence and there is a huge responsibility on the wingers to have the ability to kick the ball accurately down field and keep it in play. If a particular weakness is spotted in the defence – maybe the left wing is dodgy under the the high ball – it's exploited today with ruthless efficiency. Your outside half may try to keep a left-footed opposition full back close to the left touch line to minimise the effectiveness of his return kick. Any advantage must be taken and even the most confident of players

Kick and chase; Will
Carling in action
with Mike Catt
ready to chase in
support.

*Right:* Jonah Lomu
is taken around the
knees, to Neil
Back's delight.

under the high kick will be concerned about the sound of the opposition chasing forwards ready to bury him into the ground.

# The art of defence

Your defence in rugby is only as strong as its weakest link and opposition teams are very good at pinpointing potential areas that can be exploited in attack. You have to work together and there are three key areas that have to operate in any successful defence. Firstly, you must have speed endurance; the ability to make a tackle and then get back up on your feet ready for the next attacker. Secondly, you have to be able to react instinctively to whatever threat is being posed and ensure you are onside, behind the ball, otherwise you will give away crucial penalties for tackling an opponent or playing the ball from an offside position. Finally, every good defending team has a bit of dog in them, the refusal to back down, the will to come back snapping and snarling at the opposition heels, no matter how many attacks they launch at your line. You have to be prepared to get very physical, although self-control is important, and one man flying around making big hits is not going to be effective unless he is in communication with the rest of the defence and the whole team is operating on the same wavelength.

# The tackle

In an ideal world, every tackler is attempting to dislodge the ball and force a turnover which allows you to get hold of possession and start dictating play. In the modern game tackles have been developed with the specific aim of knocking the ball out of an opponent's arms but, if you cannot achieve this, make sure you put the man on the ground. The only way to get an opponent on the ground is to tackle him low around the ankles. I haven't seen many players able to run when their legs are being held together – not even Jonah Lomu. Big upper-body hits happen to be in vogue at the moment and when they come off it's a huge boost to the defending team and wins back the ball. However, if the ball-carrier doesn't get knocked back, he is still able to move forward because no one went for his legs.

Players have a responsibility to ensure they don't get beaten one-on-one when making the tackle and if everyone is playing their part, you become a difficult side to break down and beat. You always have to believe that the next tackle will dislodge the ball and it's a fact that one team does not dominate a match for eighty minutes. There will be long periods when all you are concentrating on is defence and maintaining that line of tacklers and you must be passionate about this thankless work. The bottom line is if you stop the opposition going forward, then you will win the match. No team in history has triumphed without scoring.

The tackle is best summed up as offensive defence, with the tackling team totally committed to putting up a wall of bodies with everyone tackling whoever comes within reach. The keys to tackling are concentration, commitment, communication and intensity. It's a discipline that, once learnt, needs constant practice but remains in the brain and gets translated into physical action during a game. There must be as much pride and ambition about your defence as attack, for without that you cannot be successful at any level. The safest and simplest tackle is the one around an opponent's ankles and this continues to be the best way of stopping someone moving forward.

We are seeing every week in England more examples of what's known in the game as the New Zealand side-step. Actually, it isn't a side-step at all, just a player determined to run right through you, like Jonah Lomu. The power work is also a way of trying to minimise the effect of a big tackle, by giving you the ability to absorb the hit. Of course, the best option is to try and keep out of the way of an oncoming tackler at all times!

# Defensive patterns

You have to go into a game with a clear idea of how you will be defending against a particular side; not that this means adopting an inflexible approach. Problems can arise and the opposition are capable of catching you, initially, off-guard. A man-on-man defence explains itself and, as a flanker, I would be looking for my opposite number, but a variation is the drift defence. This is created by each defensive player moving across the pitch covering the ball-carrier and potential receivers and attempting to cut down their space and options. It relies on the man inside you coming across with the same speed and commitment and, unless you have confidence in the rest of your defence, problems can crop up. If a team cannot get hold of the ball they become frustrated and lose their concentration and that's when various patterns of defence start to fall apart and inevitably penalties are often conceded.

# After the tackle

You stop an opponent moving forward by means of the tackle which is defined in the rules of the game as 'taking place when a player carrying the ball in the field of play is held by one or more opponents so that he is brought to the ground or the ball comes into contact with the ground. If the ball-carrier is on one knee or both knees or sitting on the ground or on top of another player on the ground he is deemed to have been brought down.'

In all those cases where the ball-carrier has in some form touched the ground after a tackle, he must immediately pass the ball, release and get up or move away. The man who makes the tackle must also release his opponent and then move away if he has also gone to the ground. You cannot play the ball after a tackle unless you have got back on your feet. This ensures we do not have a mass of players rolling around on the pitch, trying to grab hold of the ball after every tackle. Well, it should but this is, after all, rugby union and not rocket science.

It is what happens after a tackled player is put on the ground that is fundamental to the success of the game. If opponents just fall on the tackled player and stop the ball being recyled the referee has no option but to hand out penalties. The Southern Hemisphere countries have spent ages trying to come up with an agreed attitude to what happens next when a tackled player goes to ground. The aim is to reward positive actions and penalise heavily any negative attitudes, and this is what I support. We have to back the team trying to keep the momentum of an attack going, although I accept there is a danger of making it a no contest if we stop the defending team aggressively trying to steal the ball. There is nothing wrong with trying to get your hands on the opposition ball after the tackle, as long as you are on your feet and not offside. The modern game involves increasing tackling ferocity which mirrors the increase in weight and power of the players and I cannot see this changing as professionalism gives everyone the chance to work on their fitness every day of the week.

# The late tackle

This is the other side of the tackling coin and an offence that can lead to a player being given ten minutes in the sin-bin or being yellow-carded. It has given birth to one of the most used rugby jokes: the forward being penalised for a late tackle jogs over to the referee and says, 'Sorry it was late, ref, but I got there a fast as I could!' Unfortunately, the late tackle is not a laughing matter. There are, of course, hairline decisions when a tackler arrives just as the ball has been released or booted up field and, although the crowd goes mad, the referee, aided by his touch judges, weighs up the intention of the tackler and sometimes gives him the benefit of the doubt, and waves play on.

# The high tackle

This is often called 'the clothes line' because when a player is caught by a high tackle, his legs appear to swing from underneath his body, as if he had run into

Will Greenwood gets to grips with the art of tackling.

a clothes line. The high tackle, like the late tackle, is something we do not want in the game. You should tackle below shoulder-level because the head is a vulnerable area. Referees, quite rightly, crack down on offenders and a high-tackler is likely to be cautioned or sent off. Sometimes there are mitigating circumstances, such as when a tall player tries to stop a short guy and gets the tackling angle wrong. Players often throw out an arm instinctively when wrong-footed and this can catch an opponent higher on the body than intended. These are the criteria a referee uses in deciding if there was real intent to high tackle.

# The turnover

The object of every defender in a rugby match is to do whatever he can to win back the ball. The best chance of stealing the ball is in contact after a tackle. Some players, like Neil Back of England, are superb at staying on their feet at the tackle and ripping the ball off an opponent who has been tackled and gone to ground. Neil is small by comparison with other forwards and his low centre of gravity and arm strength make him well qualified for this crucial role. The key element in any turnover is that, by stealing the ball from the opposition, you immediately turn defence into attack and that can produce scores. Attacking moves are well organised and if you can break them down, the resulting confusion is a great ally. Some of the great modern tries have resulted from ball being turned over and a team on the defence suddenly being given the chance to become an attacking force that catches the opposition cold. Defensive patterns can be very tight in international rugby and there is little chance of just running through for a try at the first attempt. You often have to be patient and try to create a gap, while holding on to the ball. Nothing infuriates a coach more than to see his players working hard to create an opening and then the ball is lost because someone failed to hold on to it in contact.

# Offside

This is a critical law because it makes teams stay behind the ball, or behind your own players if they are involved in a contact situation, and creates space to allow attacks to be launched. The referee now has the help of his two touch judges who make sure that the defending team stays onside and can report any transgression by speaking into their special touch flag microphones linked to the man in the middle. Ball retention is fundamental to being successful in rugby at the moment. The team in possession sets the agenda and puts the opposition totally on the back foot. It doesn't really matter if a team does come up offside, as long as you retain the ball you could eventually score.

There are times when the ball is coming back slowly for the team in attack and they are going nowhere, with the opposition constantly offside. That's when the referee has to act quickly because frustration can build up. Every player knows that the touch judge is now playing an active role in the match and it's far better being a yard back from the offside line than taking a chance. Giving away a penalty is even more costly these days because you can gain 40 metres with a kick to touch, retain the put-in, win the line out again and make another 20 metres which really hurts the team that offended in the first place.

The professional foul isn't widespread but there are certain teams that infringe purposely to ensure they don't concede a try. It's the view that giving away three points is better than conceding seven. In the past New Zealand have often been accused of this tactic but they appear to do it so innocently.

A lack of discipline can give away penalties for offside and it can often boil down to fitness. Players get tired and sloppy in their work on the field and just one step too many costs you three crucial points when it would have been so simple just to stay onside. One of the best examples of outstanding self-control in this department was the Lions' second test victory over South Africa to clinch the 1997 series in Durban when, under the most intense pressure, we gave away only one penalty for offside in the second half. That was incredible team discipline.

# Advantage

This essentially means the same as in football and occurs when the referee has spotted an infringement but the innocent team still has possession and he is waiting to see if any meaningful advantage can be gained by letting play continue. If not, the referee calls play back for the original infringement and confusion does arise because some officials let the game go on for longer than others. Two phases of play following the offence should be enough time to decide if there is an advantage. Some officials allow just one phase to be completed. There is a classic example where the opposition knock on the ball in your 22 and one of your team kicks to touch. The referee must decide whether you would gain greater advantage if he brought play back for the knock-on and awarded a scrum. When advantage is played in open field you can score tries and it's a good law because it allows the game to flow.

There can be certain instances where a referee turns a blind eye to little incidents in order to keep the game flowing and that can cost the innocent team dearly. There are laws to be applied and if you give any rugby player an inch he will take a mile. All we are looking for is consistency from the match official. A little bit of common sense and empathy with the players can achieve a lot.

# The line out

This aspect of rugby has been fundamentally changed because the laws now allow a jumper to be lifted into the air. People claim it is no longer a contest but I disagree, although it does now favour the side throwing the ball in. Another recent change is that when a team is awarded a penalty and opts to kick the ball over the touch line, they now retain possession and can throw into the line out at the point where the ball left the pitch. Each team has recognised jumpers who compete for the ball, although anyone amongst the seven players on each side of the line out is entitled to try and win it. Spectators often wonder at the complicated calls teams work out. These usually involve a sequence of numbers in a code which they hope is impossible for the opposition to break. This literally gives your jumpers a head start, leaving the opposition guessing where the ball will go. For example, you could call 119 Blue. The last figure is odd and so the ball will be thrown to the man standing at two in our line out and Blue means that we will then drive him up field once the ball has been caught, instead of giving it to the scrum half for him to pass it out to the backs.

There is the opportunity for fast-thinking players to use the quick throw option but they can't switch balls and the ball must not have been previously touched by someone other than the player trying to put it back into play. You can throw in to one team-mate, or even to yourself, the only rule being that the ball must go at least 5 metres into play and in a straight line. This option can be a useful means of counter-attack as it usually involves the wings, the fastest men on the pitch.

# A lifter's charter

The real shift in emphasis in the line out has been from the jumper to the men lifting him because it is their responsibility to put him up and also to bring him down safely. The jumper must have total confidence in those lifters. The general idea is to look after your team-mates, to make sure they can continue to play a vital role in the rest of the game. You can now win a line out using a player who is only 6ft tall and he can beat an opponent who stands 6ft 7ins, thanks to the lifting rule. With the referees taking the view that there cannot be a contest whilst the jumper is in the air, the defending team has just two options. First they can try and steal the ball by getting their man higher and in front of the intended receiver, or they can let the opposition catch the ball and then prepare to negate their next move. They are saying, 'OK, you win the line out but we will make it very hard for you to go anywhere after that.'

# Varying the throw

The ball thrown to the back of the line out is the best for back-line moves because it is won at the nearest point to your outside half. It is logical that ball won at the front is the slowest type of ball for the backs because the scrum half has to use a longer pass to reach the No. 10 and this gives the opposition back row and three-quarters time to race up and cut down the space. You tend to use the front jumper in pressure situations when the ball must be secured and then driven up field. This option means the player throwing into the line out is trying to hit the nearest jumper and that, in theory, should cut down the margin of error. Good line-out play means getting the rhythm right and revolves around how people throw the ball in, jump to catch it and support their team-mates. Everyone has his own technique and line-out method and, through practice, you become familiar with one another's likes and dislikes and this enables you to mould into a single unit.

It's vital to recognise that it's a restart for the game but, unlike other restart situations, you can exert much greater control. You can dictate the numbers in the line out, the speed at which the ball is thrown and where exactly it will be contested. If you are under pressure in a match and have a throw into the line out inside your own 22 metre area, it's important to slow everything down and give the rest of the team time to regroup and concentrate. You would probably have everyone in the line out and throw to the front with a drive up field to ease the pressure. As you move up field, it's possible to increase the speed at which those various things happen and that helps maintain momentum and keeps the opposition on the back foot. Each player has to understand everything that is going on at any given line out, in defence or attack; it's very much a thinking man's game.

In the past referees used to turn a blind eye to what was going on at the line out because he could, nearly always, blow the whistle for some kind of offence every time the players formed up to contest the throw. Now referees are determined to give the jumper the best protection possible, although it still means you have to be streetwise. I am not suggesting anything illegal (heaven forbid!) but a nudge here and a push there can often give your side a slight advantage and disrupt the opposition ball.

# The scrum

This is the area of the game that signifies rugby for most people who don't know anything about the sport. It's the game's signature and suggests toothless, head-banded, large men getting ready to pack down. The scrum is arguably one of the most psychologically important parts of the game and it is awarded for a number of technical offences, most notably a knock-on or a forward pass. The scrum, like the line out, is a means of restarting the game and it can have a great psychological effect on the outcome of a match. I have played in very few contests in which the team under pressure in the scrum has gone on to win. The scrum is the ultimate combined physical confrontation in the game and attracts a certain kind of player – someone who enjoys going head-to-head with an opponent. It is often said that you need to be a little bit mad to play in the front row, because who in their right mind would get enjoyment from crashing into a heavily built opponent for eighty minutes! There have been serious injuries caused by collapsing scrums and everyone in the game is aware of the need for safety. Keeping the scrum from collapsing on the ground is left to the referee and you will often see penalties awarded against one of the front-row units as the referee tries to ensure the scrum does not become a problem area for the whole game. This front-row duel is often referred to as the contest within a contest, although that is usually the verdict of those involved in the battle. The rest of us tend to be as bemused about what the props and hookers are doing as the crowd. Still it keeps them happy and off the streets!

# The strength of the unit

Many people get the wrong impression about the scrum because it is seen as a battle solely reliant on the strength and technique of the front-row forwards. That's not the case, no matter what they tell you. A scrum is a complicated unit, made up of nine separate players (don't forget the scrum half) who have to work as one. The heavier scrum doesn't always have the upper hand because technique can nullify sheer weight advantage. A good little 'un can make life hell for a big 'un in the world of the rugby scrum. With the modern game demanding more from the forwards, we are having to find a balance between those players who can handle themselves in the set-piece battle and those who can roam around the pitch making tackles and handling the ball. It's no longer enough to be a great scrummaging or line-out forward and nothing else.

The scrum half must be able to feed the ball into the scrum down the middle of the tunnel formed by those warring front rows. If he puts it right under the feet of his own hooker, then a free kick is awarded to the other side. Opposition players try to upset the scrum by forcing you to wheel around and away from your intended area of attack. This involves pulling and pushing in different directions but if the scrum travels around 90 degrees the referee will order the two teams to break up and reform the scrum at the original point. This can be a frustrating part of the game for both fans and players. The sight of sixteen men spinning around in a series of messy scrums that are constantly being re-set is hardly a spectacle to make the heart soar.

All eight forwards, especially back-row players like myself, have to stay bound to the scrum until the ball has been released by the team in possession. This can either be through the No. 8 picking up the ball after it has been hooked back and travelled past the second rows to his feet, or by the No. 8 allowing the ball to pass his feet and be picked up by the scrum half. Before the law was introduced to make the back row stay bound, they would break off as soon as the ball was fed into the scrum and stand just behind their remaining five men to counter any attacking threat. That no longer happens and more space is now available.

## Inches do make a difference

Just a couple of inches forward movement by your scrum can make all the difference because it puts your team on the front foot and the opposition on the retreat, mentally and physically. It is so much easier to feed the ball out from a dominant scrum because the outside half comes on to the ball at pace and his back row are also moving foward to support the attack. In contrast, a scrum under pressure just transfers the problem like a game of pass the parcel. The scrum half is desperate to get the ball away, the outside half receives it standing still and, when he fails to get over the gain line, his own back row has to retreat before they can even think of securing the ball and making some forward movement.

It really is a great attacking platform if the scrum is working well and you can score tries from the quality of possession won in this set-piece area.

The mind-set for everyone in the scrum is to attack and as soon as you just try and absorb the pressure and survive then problems occur. Playing together as a unit gives you scrummaging confidence and it's the quality of practice that makes the difference. There can be, on average, thirty scrums every game and it's important that you are as clinical as possible in the first scrum as in the last. You also have to prepare for the unexpected because the opposition can cause you discomfort and force you to adapt your scrummaging.

I know that many people wonder why more injuries are not sustained, given the weight and power that is produced when two halves of a scrum collide. To have reached the highest level, the players will have trained to make themselves as powerful as possible and learnt the technical aspects necessary to survive in the heat of battle. I have been pushing in support of a scrum that is in terrible trouble during a game. But I have also seen the opposition scrum all over the place because the pressure was too much. There is a lot of satisfaction to be gleaned from this aspect of the game and it can lift the whole team.

# The maul

You score points in rugby by retaining possession and recycling it quickly to allow you to get in behind the opposition. The maul is not just a great big wrestling match in which each team is trying to rip the ball back for their side. Men like Dean Richards of England were expert in this area of play and used their immense upper-body strength to dominate mauls. England have been adept at using this as a major weapon because their players are skilled at setting up the maul properly, which means protecting the ball and then getting the players who bind on to the ball-carrier to drive the whole mass of bodies up field. A driving maul is a fearsome weapon and often the only option available to a defence is to make the maul collapse by dragging down opponents. This results in a penalty and a lot of frustration for the team in possession. You cannot join a maul from the side and must bind from the back or else the referee will penalise you for offside. You are not allowed to jump on top of players in the maul or drag an opponent out of the mass of bodies. It is an immensely strength-sapping area of the game and one that requires a lot of communication otherwise it becomes difficult to know exactly where the ball is amongst sixteen bodies.

The referee has a major role to play because he has to move constantly around the maul keeping an eye on where the ball is. If the maul stops moving he will allow a certain amount of time to let the team in possession feed it back to the scrum half. It must be frustrating for those watching because the ball isn't in view and all they can see is a heaving mass of bodies going around in an ever-decreasing circle. There is method, however, in this apparent madness and players have been forced to be more positive in this area because the new rules insist that the side in possession 'uses the ball or loses it'. If you have the ball in a maul but are going nowhere fast, the referee will halt play and give possession to the opposition at the resulting scrum.

Small players are useful in mauls because they can infiltrate by spotting areas of opportunity and sneak into the mass of bodies and get an arm on the ball. It's a good weapon to have in your armoury and by dominating this area of play, you can speed up or slow down play, depending on what suits you at that moment. Two or three players with the ball could suddenly break off the maul and something more dynamic is immediately created. The team in possession normally relies on their scrum half to act as the eyes of the maul because he can direct operations by shouting instructions, having weighed up the possible weaknesses in the opposition defence.

A driving maul is also a way of making the opposition commit extra players, rather than using them to stand off and prepare to act as tacklers in open play. If you can suck those players into a maul, space is created for your own attacking runners.

# The ruck

'A ruck takes place when the ball is on the ground and one or more players from each team are on their feet and in physical contact, closing around the ball between them.' Right, that's simple enough isn't it! No wonder referees and players are often bemused by what is going on in a ruck and who is actually committing an offence. Rucking, the winning of the ball with the boot, is an art form in New Zealand but sadly we are not great exponents of this in the Northern Hemisphere. Rucking, when performed properly, can free up ball and keep the momentum of an attack high, which is something we all want to see.

A ruck occurs when two players, one from each side, go to ground. Inevitably somebody is on the wrong side or has just fallen awkwardly and the boot can free the ball quickly from a tangled mass of arms and legs. You cannot use your hands in a ruck and that is why the boot must be used. If the ruck becomes a static mass of bodies, it is viewed as a pile-up and the referee will award a scrum, having first allowed time for the players to try and win the ball. Like the maul, you must join a ruck from the back and a penalty will be awarded if you drive in from the side. Continuity is something every team tries to achieve and rucking can be a vital ingredient because, when properly set up and executed, it can be as effective as a pass.

# Setting up the ruck

The player who has been tackled and falls to the floor has the responsibility of ensuring he makes the ball available in the best possible way to allow his

François Pienaar gives his Springbok team-mates a target to initiate a maul by staying on his feet.

Johan Le Roux gives Jason Leonard advice about being on the wrong side of the ruck.

team-mates to clear out the opposition and recycle possession. It comes down to correct technique, and training ground routines enable players to learn the basics properly. Being a flank forward, I have found myself in a number of compromising positions after making a tackle. The laws state that the tackler must make a real effort to get out of the way or concede a penalty. If you are lying in the way after making a tackle then, traditionally, you can expect to feel boots on your body. You can come off the pitch and appear to have been attacked by a tiger because eight pairs of metal studs do have an effect on skin and clothing. There is an unwritten law in the game that players keep their boots away from the head and ankles for obvious reasons. Being rucked is the consequence of getting yourself into the wrong place at the wrong time and if those thundering boots are not enough encouragement to get out of the way, then I don't know what is!

The opposition's intention should be to free the ball up by use of the boot, not to injure the tackler, and that is where the referee plays a crucial role. It's vital that if he feels an infringement has occurred, he gives a penalty quickly in a situation where the ball is not going to come out. Any delay leads to frustration and various countries have different attitudes about how to deal with a player on the wrong side of the ruck. When I first played in Australia, I fell on the wrong side and I had very little skin left on my back once the opposition had finished pointing out my mistake in no uncertain terms. Once you get that sorted out, it makes for a far faster match with the tackler rolling out of the way and the ball freed up for the scrum half to use and the referee keeps his whistle silent.

# 4
# Coaching

## Do we need a coach?

A coach is needed because, at whatever level you play, there must be organisation. The coach can bring a range of opinions and options and wider breadth of rugby knowledge to the squad. For many players it is an absolute must and the coach becomes a kind of mentor. The coach helps build up their confidence, as well as improving their individual skills and, most importantly, their fitness levels for what is now a very fast and powerful game at the highest level. There are many good coaches who have a lot to offer. Sometimes they are referred to as a director of rugby, director of coaching or just first-team coach but, whatever the title, the job remains the same; that is to create an environment in which each player can express himself and in which the various combinations can be melted down into a winning team formula. That environment is not just on the pitch because it has to exist all around the squad and underpins everything you do. Without that collective commitment, very little of substance can be created, no matter how hard you work. In many cases we are talking about a coaching team rather than just one individual.

I don't know why we in this country are so obsessed with responsibility for success and failure being attributed to just one man. If things go wrong, the coach gets it in the neck. But when 3 p.m. comes, he can do very little to alter the outcome of the game. It's important that the players take responsibility for what they are trying to achieve. Yes, the half-time break now allows a coach to chat to the team and he even makes substitutions throughout the game, but he cannot come on to the pitch and drive off the back of a scrum or win a line-out ball.

It is vital to see individual players making decisions under pressure and that they are comfortable with that responsibility and do not look to the coach or one or two influential players to shape the match. There is no comfort zone or hiding place in the modern game and the lazy player will be quickly found out. Anyone can do the talking in training – and I have met some great talkers in my time – but it's out on the pitch that counts. Translating all the hard work undertaken on the training pitch into something meaningful is the ultimate aim of both the coach and the players. I accept that if you watch a talented team and it's obvious that they are not operating at full throttle and the game plan is not being applied with any conviction, the role of the coach must come under the spotlight.

However, it is also true that a team doesn't become bad overnight and my own club, Wasps, is a case in point. We won the League in 1996–97 and, thanks to a combination of serious injury and a dip in form, we struggled the following season. It didn't mean our coach was to blame. Everyone has to stand up and be counted when things are not working. It is only by staying together that performances will improve.

I do wonder what is happening at other clubs where high-profile coaches are sacked because internal politics are allowed to have too great an impact, to the detriment of rugby in this country. There are people making decisions about the future of a coach who often know little about the modern game and that's a real problem. There appears to be a new tier of management in rugby that is not always having the best effect on the game as a whole.

It helps if you like the coach, although everyone has played for someone who's not their favourite character, but they get their head down for the sake of the other players. However, if the relationship between the coach and player is a harmonious one, it's more likely that we will see the best brought out and the team will greatly benefit. Confidence is crucial and if that exists between a player, his coach and the rest of the team, he will want to give absolutely everything to try and bring success to the club. It's fairly easy to identify which teams have had that in abundance and continue to benefit from this collective will to win and superb team spirit.

# Get fit

The coach has to create a framework, one tailored to the particular strengths and weaknesses of the squad. There is no point trying to achieve something that is patently beyond the capabilities of the players on the training pitch. If a coach has a squad of wonderful runners and athletic forwards, there is absolutely no point in devising a pattern of play that involves stuffing the ball up your jersey and attempting to maul and drive your way to success through the pack. The coach has to ensure that the game plan remains simple and the players who will instigate the pattern of play are supremely fit, because that is the most vital asset to any side. A coach will sit down with his fitness advisor in the summer and say, 'This is the game plan we want to follow. Are the players fit enough?' And it will be up to the fitness expert to give an honest answer. That is the starting point

My moment of league triumph – it's ours.

and once the pre-season training programme is completed the coach should have a squad of players ready to put his ideas into action.

# Pre-season training

Pre-season training is an important time for both the coaches and the players, as it becomes a time of bonding with the new faces who have arrived since the end of the last season and are bedding themselves into the squad. The coach may be new and he will need to get basic ideas across, while learning about the character and personality of the squad he has inherited. It's a great time for any club because you are earning the respect of your team-mates through hard work, and the fitness advisor will have come up with a punishing schedule of runs and power work to test even the fittest member of the squad.

Coaches bring in new players for specific reasons and they have been identified by the club as being able to fill a hole that exists in the squad. It's vitally important that whoever is brought in must be able to blend into the existing family set-up because that is what we are talking about in a first-team squad. You are going to spend a lot of time together over the coming years and no club can afford to have divisive elements in the first-team squad. Fitness is monitored by the sadistic advisor for the rest of the season but at this pre-season point he hands what's left of the players back to the coach and the rugby practice is initiated.

Some coaches prefer to integrate work with a rugby ball as fitness is being built up, while others opt to stick to just fitness for a while. The coach has to stimulate the players in his training sessions and it's a fine line between necessary repetition to make something second nature and mind-numbingly boring sessions that just seem to be a repeat of everything that's gone before. The old adage that practice makes perfect is still true and if you hit fifty or sixty scrums in training, you will get it right in a match. I am a firm believer in Gary Player's view that he seemed to be luckier at golf the harder he practised.

# Getting switched on

It's very important to focus on the quality of training rather than quantity, especially now that the game is professional and we train together nearly every day. A coach has to be conscious that the squad is not practising just for the sake of practice. It's true that you can achieve much more in a concentrated thirty-minute session, with everyone switched on and performing the drills at high speed, than trotting around for three hours at half pace. Confidence has to be generated on the training pitch and it's often the case that players go into a match in the wrong frame of mind because they haven't switched on in training. You have to be able to use a mental switch that is flicked to on when a session starts and then turned to off when it ends, because that ensures time is not wasted. It is possible for the coach to have a laugh with the players in training, as long as you first recognise that there is a serious purpose every time you go on to the pitch for a session. There is real satisfaction in taking a move from the practice pitch into a match and making it work successfully, because it means you have outfoxed the opposition through collective effort and application. It's a public pat on the back for the squad.

## Changing tactics

Nine times out of ten the ideas people come up with are good but it all comes down to the execution and players must have the confidence at training to give an honest verdict. If the coach believes a tactic can be successful but the front five forwards disagree, then both sides of the argument have to be heard. There is no point going on to the pitch unhappy with an instruction from the coach because, if you don't believe it will be a success, no one else is going to have faith.

With the amount of rugby being played and the increased use of television and video cameras, a move that works one week is not always likely to succeed seven days later because the spies will have noted how it was created and evolved a plan to nullify it. The onus is on the coach and the players to be inventive throughout the season and everyone steals everybody elses ideas. You have to keep opponents guessing.

## The myth about game plans

Winning line-out ball and dominating the scrums are parts of any game plan and fundamentals that every side attempts to achieve. There is a pattern within which you play and it's all about going forward – as simple as that. A game plan is making decisions at the right time and having the ability to execute them properly. Northern Hemisphere rugby has to get rid of the idea that in certain areas of the pitch you only have one option, such as if you are in your own 22 a kick must be the right choice. The right option could be a kick to touch or downfield to make the defence turn, but if their wingers have dropped back, expecting the boot to be put to ball, why not exploit the space that is created in their defence and keep the ball alive? That would be the right decision at that moment, but if your game plan is too rigid the opposition will recognise that very quickly and adapt their tactics accordingly.

Remaining flexible is the key and any rigid game plan will leave you floundering if it is patently failing to make any impression on the opposition. It's very important that a team does not come off the pitch after eighty minutes saying, 'If only we had done this or that,' because it's within the power of every player during a game to make decisions that shape the team's tactics. New Zealand are the best at this flexible approach. If your pattern is not breaking down the opposition, that information has to be communicated through the team and everyone has to start playing smart football and work out an alternative. It doesn't come down to just one or two key players, because they may be at the bottom of a ruck when the ball comes back; the options are to go left, right or straight head. It's as simple as that.

# Half-time

Half-time used to be a matter of minutes with the coach having to send out his advice through the guy carrying the plate of oranges or the physio. It's important to keep the intensity of the game high. We already have too many stoppages. We have seen the problem with American football where every play is shouted into the ear of the quarter-back by the relevant touch-line coach and you end up playing by numbers in between commerical breaks for television. The new ten-minute half-time allows a rugby coach to talk at length to his players (or if you're John Hart – the referee) and address any problems that have arisen in the first half. That input can affect the outcome of a game, although I often feel that if your team is winning you would rather keep the momentum going. Under the new system the time allows a losing team to gather its thoughts, and players to refuel the body with specific fluids and re-energise the mind for the forty minutes of rugby still to be played.

The use of substitutes is an important factor and the coach may want to send out new faces in the second half to give the team momentum and boost one aspect of the play. Substitutes are a very good idea and in the old days the fact that you could not replace anyone added to the image of hard men who would stay on despite all kinds of problems. With the advent of professionalism, coaches were wary of taking players off because it used to be viewed as a sign that the person coming off had under-performed. That is not the case and we have to accept that subs can play a vital part in a team's strategy. I don't believe it cheapens international caps and, as a sub, you can have a major impact on the game, no matter how long you are on the pitch. If something is not going right, a coach can now make a change before the game is lost.

Players are starting to accept this is now part of the game; if a card goes up on the touch line with your number on it, you get off and someone else does the business. The crowd enjoy the longer break. They get to talk about various incidents and look forward to the next half and speculate about the final result. When you sit down to dinner you don't have all three courses on the table at the same time. There is time to savour each properly. American football is like a banquet that goes on far too long; rugby union needs to be enjoyed at the right pace and, I think, we have now got the correct period between halves.

# The post-match debrief

Each team is different and so is every coach. How they deal with the immediate aftermath of a game is vital. You cannot enter a dressing room with preconceived ideas about what you are going to say. It has to be relevant to what has just happened and on many occasions it may be right just to let the players be. The coach might opt to wait a couple of hours because the dressing-room area, particularly after an international, can be pretty chaotic.

Two players will have to go for mandatory drug testing and that can be a really frustrating time, as your body is dehydrated yet they need you to provide a specimen. Other players are doing interviews for the television, while four or five could be warming down in the gym we have under the West Stand at

Dean Richards in his new role as a coach at Leicester.

Twickenham. There are times, when you have lost, that you need to show you are all still together and that may be the moment when a captain reflects on the performance or the coach has a quiet word. There are no hard and fast rules.

I have given, and sat through, a number of pre- and post-match talks; there are times when each player has to sit there and listen to a few home truths because, in sport, players can under-perform, as England proved in Paris in 1998. It can be very personal and it does hurt but that's all part of being a member of a rugby team. I have been sitting alongside players who have made major howlers that have cost the team victory but it's never as simple as the media portray the situation. Our kicker may have missed a penalty to win the match but he should not have been put into the position of having to rescue the side. We should have, collectively, won the game before that kick came along. This is a team game and there is a responsibility we all share in the triumphs and defeats. No player should be made the scapegoat, though it does happen and you feel for them deeply. You are in this together, and if you all share in the joy of victory, then you must accept your part of the burden of defeat.

# Reward for hard work

An enormous amount of work went into allowing me to walk up those couple of wooden steps and hold the Courage League trophy aloft at Northampton at the end of the 1996–97 season. So many people, on and off the pitch, showed a level of consistency and excellence that no one could claim the title was won by luck. A deep sense of satisfaction comes from realising that as a club you have achieved something very special and no matter how big or small each individual's contribution has been, you are all able to stand together and yell, 'We are the best!' It's a lovely feeling and one that becomes addictive. In order to realise how good that is you have to be the team in the other dressing room.

In every avenue of sport, you get downsides and it's how you as an individual react in adversity that contributes to making you and the team great. England losing to France in Paris in 1998 in the short term was catastrophic, in the long term the mental scars left by that match will take me forward to victory.

# Caught on camera

There is a place for video analysis in the game because it can help players improve and develop individual skills. Being self-critical is much easier when your own performance is there in moving colour on the screen and all the good and bad things from the last match can be pored over. Sometimes you come off the pitch believing that your performance was good and then the video shows you knocked on twice and lost the ball in contact once. There is always room for improvement and the video tapes allow a player to build up a library of performances during a season or even a career, so that he can chart the areas that are getting better or worse. It is important for a player to work on the areas of his game that need improving. Too many players only practice the skills they are really good at.

I also like to watch tapes of my opposite number, particularly at international level, in order to get a feel for how he plays in given situations, whether he prefers to come off his left or right foot when running with the ball, and how he fits into the opposition's pattern of play. It also helps build up the anticipation for a match and gets the adrenalin going.

You have to be open-minded and remember Hannibal won all his wars by doing things the opposition didn't expect (just ask those elephants). So I don't forget that the guy I will be facing will have been looking at the same video clips I am studying. The reason England almost beat the great New Zealand team of 1997 was because we did exactly the opposite of what they expected. They had studied the videos of previous England games and never thought we would run from the first minute. They probably expected plenty of box kicks from the scrum half and No. 10 and that, if they came flat and fast to make the midfield tackles, we would not pass the ball but just kick. You can watch endless videos of a team and then they can come out and play in a completely different way. Analysis is important but you must acknowledge that teams can change and you have to expect the unexpected.

# The coach's will

Disagreements with the way a coach or manager is doing his job are bound to arise, but he has to be allowed to do it the way he believes is best. A lot of critics said Andy Robinson was crazy initially to leave out England full back Matt Perry for Bath's Heineken Cup final with Brive, but he was proved absolutely correct, with Jon Callard slotting over the kicks to win the Cup. The following week, in different playing circumstances, Perry came into the side for JC and played superbly and that was the coach's call and sometimes it's a very hard one to make. Who would have expected New Zealand to leave Jonah Lomu out of their test team when the winger came back from injury? John Hart, the All Blacks coach, was happy that Glen Osborne was the man in form and left Lomu on the bench to the amazement of many. Again, it was the coach's call and he was correct.

Another player who has swapped playing for coaching – Andy Robinson at Bath.

# Backing the coach

The coach lives and dies on playing results while the players are judged more on performance and that will continue to be the case. Clubs in England now have boards of directors who want success because they are investing so much money in the game. If a coach is dismissed it does have a huge effect on the club because that individual will have built up strong bonds with the players and earned respect. I always talk to my squad about the responsibility that comes with the contracts we have with the club. It is often the case that the first game after a coach has been sacked brings a major performance out of the team because those players feel the need to prove themselves to whoever has taken over the reins.

It may have been the case that the players had not lost faith in the sacked coach, but they were, for whatever reason, under-performing. Clubs have to realise that there's no point making a change just for the sake of change because there are no guarantees. It's the long term that's imporant and fortunes can turn very quickly in sport when a struggling team suddenly puts together a run of wins and moves up the table. In that situation some other club coach's head is put on the chopping block, not yours. There is a real danger when panic measures are taken and then possibly regretted, e.g. Leicester and Bob Dwyer.

# 5

# Coming through the ranks

## …to the back row

I was fortunate to attend Ampleforth School where John Wilcox, the former England full back, teaches and also coaches the young players. The route that I followed, which eventually took me to Cape Town where I sat on the bench for England against South Africa in the famous Newlands stadium in 1994, can still be followed, even in this professional era. Having played rugby aged eight years old for Staines RFC minis, I started off at Ampleforth as a wing and enjoyed my time waiting for the forwards to agree to let us have the ball in matches! Eventually, my increasing height brought a suggestion from Frank Booth, my coach at U16 level, that I should think about a switch to the back row and No. 8 in particular. I was happy to try this new role, which meant the ball would arrive at my feet at scrums and I could take a much more active part in the game. That first match as a member of the back row went well and I was hooked for life.

## Bending ears

Unfortunately, other people had different views. The county championship, before the advent of leagues, was and still is an important part of English rugby and not just at senior level. I was given a trial by Middlesex Schools (my pre-Ampleforth qualification) at U18 level which was the standard route players followed if they hoped to win selection for England at that age level. I got into the side as a second row. I haven't revisited that particular position since my schools rugby days and my ears are delighted by that fact. Everyone believes their particular chosen position is the best in the team and, over the years, I have come to love anywhere in the back row. When second rows start going on about what a great job they can do in the scrum with their heads jammed between two ample front-row frames, I just start to glaze over. Cauliflower ears are an unfortunate occupational hazard for any forward. So far, so good. However, the position in which I played in those early years was dictated by the various selection panels that existed at schools and county levels and I had no option but to agree to jam my head between two front-row team-mates and dream of England selection – hopefully in the back row.

I was picked as a middle jumper and second row for London Schools and it gave me my first sighting of a player I was to get to know very well. He was Simon Shaw, the Wasps and England lock, and even at that age he was gigantic. It was hard enough to see our own hooker with him standing at number two in the line out, let alone try and keep the opposition away from our ball. I went for an England Schools trial as a second row at Trent College and managed to score a try, and felt I contributed well round the field. But this was not good enough for the selectors, which I found, and still do, rather baffling.

The President of the Schools told me I wasn't fit enough to play for England – another point I could not accept. He often comes up to me for a chat now that I am the England captain. At least he has the grace to look sheepish whenever we talk about that verdict. But it made me determined never to be put in that position again when taking part in a big trial and I trained even harder to give myself a shot at the team next time so whatever he said, it certainly worked. I played for Middlesex Colts and won the divisional championship playing for London Colts, when the competition had real significance. Then my first taste of international rugby came as the England Colts No. 8 – at least I had escaped from the second row for the time being.

# Wasps and England U21

Having got into the England set-up as a flanker I thought there would be a natural progression into the Wasps first team. However, Dean Ryan, a player and coach of real ability and one of the major influences on me as a player, was the Wasps captain and No. 8, so I reverted to the blind side flanker role I had made my own at Ampleforth. I had to toughen up and learn exactly what being a first-class rugby player meant and Dean certainly helped in my education. It was thoroughly enjoyable. At U21 level I was persuaded by Surrey that, as I was now living on the other side of the Thames, I should join their squad rather than Middlesex. As many of my friends at Wasps were already with that county, I agreed to the move. It was a timely switch because we won the U21 county championship and that led on to London and England U21 selection.

I was plucked from the Wasps squad, thanks to Dick Best, and given the unique opportunity to be part of England's 1993 Rugby World Cup Sevens squad and we won the tournament at Murrayfield to the great surprise of everyone in the English game. After that marvellous occasion I was picked to tour Australia with an England U21 side that reads all these years later like the 1998 senior England squad. In fact, the England back row that took on New Zealand at Twickenham in November 1997 – Tony Diprose, Richard Hill and myself – was the same unit as the U21 back row in Sydney for the test match we won against Australia. The only difference was the numbers we wore on our shirts. I was open side flanker, Richard was No. 8 and Dippy handled the blind side. Also in the team were Will Greenwood, Kyran Bracken, Mike Catt, Simon Shaw, Mark Regan and Austin Healey. Those in that U21 team who haven't been capped are playing for the England A side or in first-class teams in England.

That tour was an important step forward for all concerned and it's just a shame that it took so long for many of those players to be recognised at senior England level. The U21 side proved an England team could go to Australia and win a test match, something the full England side has yet to achieve in that country. With the current senior England set-up, I don't believe we would have a situation in which U21 players would be ignored by the selectors.

# Capped twice

When the Australian tour finished, I returned to Wasps and played in the first three league matches as an open side flanker, eventually being dropped after playing poorly against Leicester when Neil Back outplayed me pretty comprehensively. Despite this setback, I was picked by London Division against the North and we managed a narrow win, with me again in the open side flanker's role. That game was the criterion for selection for the London Division against the All Blacks at Twickenham the following week and I was dropped in favour of Rory Jenkins because the selectors felt they needed a more physical presence at No. 7. It was a very disappointing situation because the All Blacks only tour every four years, so I had missed my chance to test myself againt the best in the world and had to watch the game from the Twickenham stands. With hindsight, I can see the reasons why I was dropped, but at the time it was hard to take as I had only ever been dropped once before in my career and that was a week earlier! When it rains it pours and I felt pretty low as their reason for dropping me – I wasn't physical enough – was because I had played so little first team rugby. Who's fault was that?

I learnt very quickly that at some stage in your rugby career, you get shafted by the selectors and it could come in your first or your hundredth game, but when it comes you must bite your lip, be professional and get on with it. I watched London getting crushed by the All Blacks and just wished I could have been out there for a match that didn't look that physical and was very fast. A twenty year old like myself could have handled that. The whole

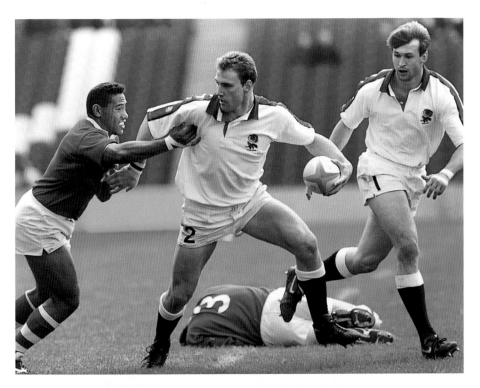

*Above:* Playing for England in the 1993 World Cup Sevens with Justyn Cassell in support.

*Left:* Richard Hill (facing camera) tries to look interested in my team talk.

*Facing page:* Simon Shaw uses that great height to good advantage.

experience made me more determined, although at Wasps I was finding the No. 7 role was a problem. I was coming up against other open sides with two hundred or so games under their belts, people like Backy, Peter Winterbottom, Andy Robinson and Gary Rees, while I had just three games to my name.

I had to find a position that suited me and that meant time out of the Wasps first team. I was given the blind side role and realised it was vital to start getting credibility in the club game. I put thoughts about being included in any representative squads to the back of my mind and that is why it was such a welcome boost to be included in one of Geoff Cooke's final England training squads before he quit as team manager. That was in November 1993 and came a month after the disappointment of not facing New Zealand for London.

# England squaddie

I turned up for the session alongside a number of Wasps guys, including Jeff Probyn and Rob Andrew, and I knew this was great opportunity to learn a hell of a lot from the best players in the country. I didn't feel daunted because I had been around pretty high-profile players at Wasps and by following the England representative ladder. A number of those players had made the same journey and reached this same point. It does prepare you for the full squad and what might happen once you hit that new level. Before the 1994 England tour to South Africa in the summer, I was given two A games.

# England A

My first appearance came as a replacement in Paris in a side that featured a number of players who had been dropped after the senior international with Scotland. The A team was getting hammered and the only guy I thought was playing anywhere near his ability was Neil Back and he eventually scored a deserved try. While I was sitting on the bench, an RFU committee man came along and put his arm on my shoulder and asked who was out there playing in the England back row. It was nice to know he was really in touch with the game! I came on with Darren Garforth with five minutes to go and I enjoyed my first brief taste of rugby at that level. Then I was picked to start against Ireland at Donnybrook and we won that match. It was a mixture of youth and experience and who should be in the England A second row but Simon Shaw, my old partner from the London Schools side. It was that match which helped win me a place on the England tour to South Africa in 1994, which was always going to be a difficult trip, with everyone having one eye on the World Cup to be staged there the following year.

# To South Africa with England

Getting the South African trip was a surprise because it went against previous tours which had not featured up-and-coming players. People have a lot of opinions about Jack Rowell as England manager and coach but he did have one eye on the future and took players to South Africa who were not established test stars. I was delighted to be part of an England tour and it made me realise I was now in the big time and amongst the élite players. There were great characters like Brian Moore and Stuart Barnes in the tour party, although not everyone got on with each other. I wasn't about to arrive with all guns blazing and was prepared to look and listen to what was going on. I kept my head down and tried to absorb all the information and experiences that came along. I was a twenty year old who didn't feel out of place, but I knew that I had to be a quick learner. There was a large Wasps contingent in the tour party, including Damian Hopley who was also a member of the England Sevens team that won the World Cup and I felt at home with Hoppers who is a good tourist. Barnesy was also good company and a man who knew when to let his hair down.

The tour opened my eyes because, for various reasons, it was quickly allowed to develop into two separate teams and I felt that was a real weakness. The two rarely crossed over. I played in the first match against Orange Free State on a bone-hard cricket pitch in Bloemfontein. We lost the match and then the 'first' team was beaten by Natal which meant we were without a win after two weeks in South Africa and that was a major blow which put us on the back foot. The first rule of touring – always win your opening game – had not been followed. We spent a lot of time training as separate teams, too, which made it difficult to enjoy any time with the likes of Will Carling and Rob Andrew, and although we travelled together, our self-imposed apartheid persisted. I believe the same kind of thing had happened on the 1993 Lions tour in New Zealand. Subsequent tours have learnt from the mistakes of those two trips.

Having played in the first game, I didn't get another chance until the South Africa A match at Kimberley, and that meant two weeks of doing nothing but training and trying to support those players who were involved in the games. No one bothered to tell me what was going on and there was a danger that I could have just drifted along. The initial joy of being selected for the tour evaporated and it became patently clear that, once you were on tour, no one stands on ceremony. If you play well, they pick you. I wanted the opportunity to prove I could be an important part of the tour and the game in Kimberley was a turning point for the whole party.

Before the A game, Dean Ryan, who is a better captain and player than people will ever give him credit for, got together with Steve Bates and Stuart Barnes and decided how to win the game. In a sense they took ownership of the game and we really went at South Africa A in way that had not happened on tour until that match. We rattled a few cages and, were it not for a few dodgy refereeing decisions and errors on our part – one glaring one by myself – we should have won. The Kimberley match contained everything – good tries, a bit of fighting, a hostile atmosphere and even a moment of humour amidst the tension. They had just scored a try and we all huddled around Dean Ryan under the posts so that he could issue another call to arms. Steve Ojomoh, the No. 8, was absolutely gagging for air when, suddenly, an orange hit him straight on the nose and there was nothing we could do but burst out laughing. Steve had one of those tours where he just attracted attention and there was something happening to him every match. He played in almost every match, too, because of injuries to Dean Ryan and Dean Richards. A new tone was set for the tour at Kimberley and a few days later England thrashed South Africa in the first test at Loftus Versfeld in Pretoria with Rob Andrew having a dream match.

# The Battle of Boet Erasmus

Then came Boet Erasmus Stadium at Port Elizabeth and the infamous battle with Eastern Province who at that point were coached by Alex 'Grizz' Wyllie. I knew they would be rucking anything that came within reach of their studs. How right I was. Having said that, I wasn't quite prepared for what was about to happen and when it did start to go off, I looked around my team and knew which side I was happy to be on. We had men like Dean Ryan and Graham Dawe who had earned respect from opponents for their uncompromising play, the pack was big and aggressive, and we had talented backs like the in-form Paul Hull to cut through for tries.

Right from the kick off, they came steaming into us when we failed to secure possession properly and it was pretty clear none of the Eastern Province boys were playing the ball. I took a knee in the back at the first ruck and there were fists flying all over the place, including Dean Ryan's which resulted in my old mate breaking a thumb. He tried to stay on the field with just one good arm and, eventually, Tim Rodber took over and that proved to be a fateful decision as he was later sent off while captaining the side. That wasn't until the second half, by which time we had secured victory and they started to lose it badly after the game had teetered on a knife-edge for most of the time.

I don't have a problem with rucking and if I am on the wrong side of the ball, I expect to be rucked out of the way; it helps let players know when they are overstepping the mark and stopping release of the ball. But I do remember one ruck in Port Elizabeth where the ball had come out on our side and reached Paul Hull's hands on the wing, yet one of their forwards was still doing a bit of tap-dancing on my back. Nowadays, I would probably sort it out myself, but this was my first senior tour and, thankfully, Dawesy and few others came to my aid.

Dean Ryan leading from the front against South Africa in Kimberley.

My roomy Graham Dawe in the thick of it as usual.

Jon Callard received a horrific cut to his head, very close to an eye, which was an absolute disgrace from a player who was to reappear against the Lions in 1997. That was an act of violence that has no place in rugby and it could have been life-threatening. I remember running towards a ruck with Dawesy and an opposition player just came up and kneed him in the back. The referee had no control of the game. Anything like it today and players would be cited and banned.

Dawesy is one of the nicest people I met on the tour. They roomed us together because I was the youngest and he was one of the more experienced players in the party. We had ten days sharing a hotel room in Durban at the start of the trip. I could not have wished for a better room-mate to help me settle down into my first senior tour. Instead of spending time with his mates from all the years of being an England player, Dawesy spent time with me. That is something I have never forgotten and it was a great introduction to the set-up.

You have to remember, too, that Dawesy had sat on the bench more than thirty times watching Brian Moore wearing the No. 2 jersey, yet his enthusiasm and work rate in training never wavered. He was ambitious and energetic at a time when you could understand a player in his position being bitter and bitchy. I have a great respect for Dawesy as a player. They don't make hookers like him and Mooro any more – they were just different from the rest.

Eastern Province that day did exactly what they set out to do; they got stuck into England and caused so many problems that the build up to the second test was totally overshadowed by the sending off of Tim Rodber and the injury to Jon Callard. We had to deal with a whole series of problems that took our concentration off winning the series in South Africa and, in hindsight, it was a mistake to let the photographers into the dressing room after the match to take pictures of various injuries, including the stud marks on my back. I wasn't too worried about my back, our only real concern was for Jon Callard after that disgraceful incident. I was told to turn around and let the cameras take pictures, but when you think about desperate acts of rugby violence, you don't think about Dallaglio's back, because that is something that can happen and I have taken plenty of shoeings since that match. All the publicity that the match generated only helped to distract the squad leading up to that second test in Cape Town.

# On the bench at Cape Town

For me, the week started to take on real significance because, having begun the tour as the new boy, wondering if I would ever get a game, I was now in line to be handed a place on the bench. Dean Richards had a calf strain and, with Dean Ryan nursing that broken thumb, Steve Ojomoh was elevated to the team and

I took his spot on the replacements bench. It was clearly going to be an explosive test because South African pride had been hurt by our win in Pretoria and they were always going to come at us with a frenzied attack. Sitting on the bench was a wonderful experience and preparing for the match generated a mixture of excitement and fear, which allows adrenalin to kick in. I just wanted to be involved although I realise, looking back, that the squad wasn't in the right frame of mind to face the Springboks, thanks to the legacy of Port Elizabeth. We were hit by a very physical Springbok side that kicked the ball in the air and really piled into us; they recognised an opportunity for revenge. Ben Clarke was injured early in the game and appeared to be flat out, so I took my tracksuit off, expecting to have to play. I can still remember the adrenalin rush at the thought of entering the game. In the event I didn't come on. We lost at Newlands and we all felt a real disappointment at not winning the series.

However, for me there was considerable personal satisfaction. I had been part of a huge learning curve and when I compared the point I had started the tour from and where I had finished, I could be pleased with my first England experience. I was totally committed to doing whatever was necessary to win that first cap. I still have the No. 17 jersey I wore in Cape Town, and it reminds me of a day I will never forget. I had travelled a long way from Match Field at Ampleforth to Newlands in Cape Town via county championship matches as an U16 player. It is a path that could disappear in the professional era, but that does not mean we should ignore the county game.

# The county game

In the 1990s the role of the counties has changed, particularly at senior level where I was first noticed. I was selected for Middlesex against Cornwall in the county championship semi-final played at the famous Redruth ground with its Hellfire Corner. I played with fellow Wasps Rob Lozowski and Mark Rigby at an early point in my career and the atmosphere the Cornish supporters created was unlike anything I had experienced hitherto. It wasn't quite like Newlands, but never underestimate the passion of a Cornish crowd who know they are just one game away from what they consider to be their birthright, a day out at Twickenham for the county championship final. We lost the game 17–16 and I thoroughly enjoyed the day in a Middlesex side coached by Andy Keast, who later went off to be director of rugby at Natal and then accepted the same role with Harlequins. The county championship did have a place and still has in the game. It was certainly a useful launching pad for my career and has helped many hundreds of players to realise their rugby dreams.

# 6
# Discipline

Rugby, by its very nature, is a game played right on the edge of physical violence. I have played in a some great games where the hits have been heavy but totally legal and that should always be the case. Unless you play rugby with controlled aggression, you are asking for trouble. The game cannot afford to let those who are only interested in cheap shots off the ball continue to play a part in the sport.

Every season seems to feature a major incident of foul play at the highest level and with the arrival of professionalism, the stakes are that much higher for the aggressor and his victim. A bad injury caused by the boot, fist or head can result in a loss of earnings and a claim for compensation. This is a serious consideration. Every player must realise that by an act of foul play they could jeopardise an entire playing career – theirs. Clubs now have the ability to cancel the contract of a professional player if he fails to keep to his part of the legally binding bargain. I am sure that recent legal cases will be repeated time after time as the disciplinary side of the sport is brought up to speed to ensure it operates properly in a professional age.

Despite high-profile cases of foul play, I don't believe that by making the game professional it has become more violent. This was one of the arguments put forward by those who wanted the sport to remain amateur but they obviously had not leafed through old press cuttings. There have been incidents of foul play ever since the sport was created. Many more acts of violence went unreported in the pre-television era when coverage was restricted to black-and-white photographs, print media and radio. Within the sport there was an it's-all-part-of-the-game attitude in previous decades, which swept various incidents under the carpet. I have spoken to players who were involved in the game in the seventies and they insist there were far more off-the-ball incidents than in today's rugby; it's just that no one was that interested in club rugby, reducing the number of potential witnesses.

Rugby heads towards the millennium with a fantastic opportunity to broaden its spectator base and ensure that the professional game is a financial success. When I first started at Wasps, we only played at Sudbury, our spiritual home, which is now our training resource centre. Now Loftus Road, the magnificent stadium which is also home to QPR, is where we stage all our major games. Before our link-up with QPR, the Wasps regulars would either try to squeeze into the tiny main stand at Sudbury or escape the rain under the temporary roof on the other stand. Otherwise, it was bring an umbrella with you for a day on the concrete terraces. Our loyal fans now enjoy an all-seater stadium with catering facilities and toilets that are light years away from Sudbury.

It is all designed to create a family atmosphere, one that will ensure dads and mums will want to bring their children to watch us in action. They do not want their kids to watch incidents of violence on the pitch. That is why there is a massive responsibility on players to maintain self-control while still playing the game to the limit of their physical capabilities. No one wants to see the game watered down by draconian laws because you would lose the very essence of the sport. It comes down to us, the players, to set the right standards of behaviour and if we get it right on and off the field, the game will grow, fed by positive coverage and increasing crowds.

# Wiring the touch judge

The arrival of television cameras and video means that very few instances of foul play at the highest level go undetected. Every game contains incidents that the referee spots, but many others are missed because the man with the whistle doesn't have eyes in the back of his head. He gets accused of many things, but that's not one of them! Spectators may have been wondering why touch judges appear to be chewing the tops of their flags at various times. This is because they are wired for contact with the referee and all they are doing is ensuring they are speaking as close as possible to the microphone because the crowd noise can be absolutely deafening. Touch judges can now flag for foul play, indicate other offences and also inform the referee when backs are creeping up offside.

They can have a major and salutory impact on the game by insisting that the backs stay behind the offside line. There is nothing more frustrating for a team than to retain possession through a series of plays and then find the space you have created out wide is ruined because the opposition backs have come up offside and the ref hasn't spotted the offence. Persistent offside kills rugby as a spectacle. Any player will push it to the absolute limit – I don't claim to be a saint in this respect myself – so it's down to the referee to set out his stall very early on and make it abundantly clear that he will not allow players to hang around offside, and the touch judges are now an accepted extension in this war against offside. That is why you will see them pacing out the required distance the backs of the defending team must be at line outs and when penalties and free kicks are awarded. As players we have become used to looking to the touch line to check if we are back the required 10 metres and the touch judge gives us a thumbs up when he is happy.

It is becoming more common for off-the-ball incidents of foul play to be spotted by the touch judge, because the referee is busy following the ball and his lines of sight are often obstructed by the thirty players careering around the pitch. Touch judges have an important role but they must be consistent, as their proximity to the crowd leaves them open to constant verbal abuse. We have seen disgraceful instances in football where linesmen have been physically and verbally assaulted by fans but that has, thankfully, not happened in rugby at the highest level. There are instances of spectators getting involved in unacceptable behaviour at lower levels in the game and those people need to be kept away from the sport. The majority of attention is focused on the very top of the game but violence at any level, on or off the pitch, must be eradicated.

# Mad dads

I am concerned about reports of overzealous parents making fools of themselves at mini-rugby matches where they allow enthusiasm for a son or daughter's sporting morning to boil over. It sets a terrible example for those children playing rugby and creates an atmosphere that the game does not want or deserve. Players like Jeremy Guscott and I started in the mini sections of clubs and it gave us a wonderful introduction to the game. Anyone who has visited Richmond Athletic Ground on a Sunday morning cannot fail to be impressed with the commitment and support given by hundreds of parents who bring their kids along every weekend for mini-rugby training and matches. The sheer joy on the faces of the participants makes it all worthwhile, so it's even more important that the parents remember why they are there in the first place. Supporting your child is important, but why embarrass him or her with your lack of self-control? What kind of example are you setting your children by shouting foul and negative words from the touch line and getting involved in verbal, and heaven forbid, physical arguments with other parents or coaches? There is a real danger of parents trying to act out sporting careers they never had through their children and that is a very unhealthy scenario for all concerned. It's a mistake I never intend to make in whatever field my daughter Ella chooses to follow.

# Respect for the referee

The game was stunned when Neil Back, the Leicester flanker, was banned for six months. It wasn't the ban that shocked everyone but the offence – allegedly pushing the referee to the ground at the end of the Pilkington Cup final with Bath. It's often said, and loses nothing by repetition, that there would be no game without the referee. You could still have thirty players trotting out but without a ref the exercise is, quite literally, pointless. All three officials, the ref and his two touch judges, operate as a team these days and can receive match fees at the highest level. As the game has become faster and more complicated for the players, it has also increased in difficulty for the officials. The greater powers given to touch judges are an example of this fact and there have even been calls for two referees on the pitch. This is taking it a bit far and I cannot see that ever happening. We have enough debate about differences in interpretation from one game to another, so imagine the potential confusion with two officials on the same pitch!

# Chatting up the ref

I am half-Italian and admit that this emotional side of my personality sometimes comes out on the pitch and I make my unhappiness with various refereeing decisions very plain, though not so plain as to incur a reverse penalty if I can help it! It's the way I play the game and I cannot change. As captain of the team it's vital to respect the referee but that does not mean you cannot have a good relationship which allows plenty of positive dialogue during a game. Remember, we are all playing this game for personal enjoyment and that also goes for the man with the whistle. He has to be a rugby nut to put up with the flak from the fans!

Brian Campsall shows Leicester's Richard Cockerill the yellow card.

You are not allowed to abuse the referee and that is absolutely right. Football referees have to deal with verbal abuse from players in every match and you don't have to be an expert lip reader to realise this fact while watching any televised match. We have a different attitude to our match officials and dissent leads to a yellow or red card which is also absolutely right. Once you start eroding the position of the referee, you are on the slippery slope.

# Interpreting the rules

Because the game is now played by professionals, the natural extension is to have professional referees. The International Board is actuely aware of the need to raise and maintain refereeing standards around the world and that is why we have Southern Hemisphere officials appointed for test matches in the North and vice versa. Anything that helps to bring about an agreed application of the laws gets my vote. Currently, we still have to find out who is going to referee our matches at club and test level so that we can prepare for that style of control. Certain countries allow various aspects of the game to be refereed more liberally than others and this causes problems when Northern Hemisphere teams play in the South. The Southern countries make the same point when they come here and the problems of interpretation continue to frustrate officials, coaches and players. Rugby has one set of rules, yet they appear to allow myriad different interpretations.

At club and international level we study videos of the referee to get an idea of what particular areas he likes to concentrate on; one ref may be hot on lineout barging or offside in midfield and that's useful information. You cannot control the referee and it's a case of minimising the potential problems you create for yourself on the pitch. During a match it's vital to appreciate how the referee is going to apply the laws at key areas such as ruck, maul, line out, scrum and offside, and players need to be conscious of what is going on around them. You have to be alert because there is no point complaining about it after the event. Teams in the past have been guilty of coming off after a defeat and moaning that the referee did not officiate as they expected.

For example, in the Northern Hemisphere if you get your body under the ball-carrier in a ruck, then you win the put-in to the scrum because the ball did not reach the ground. In the Southern Hemisphere it doesn't matter if the ball is on the ground – as the law states – the put-in goes to the team going forward, who were trying to do something positive. The letter of the law states that the North is right but common sense tells us that the South is right. Some referees like the ball put in to the middle of the scrum while others are less bothered as long as it's used quickly. The referee has a job to do and he will not be changing his actions to accommodate you. It's up to you to adapt to him.

# 7
# Shooting ourselves in the foot

The Rugby Footall Union controls the game in England and the arrival of professional rugby in August 1995 required everyone involved in the sport suddenly to come to terms with a new era. Not surprisingly, it took time and is still taking time, for all the ramifications of that momentous decision to be understood. For those attending the press conference in a Paris hotel which signalled the move to professionalism, the news came as a complete shock. That feeling was mirrored around the sport and the International Board, who administer the game world wide, appeared to catch everyone on the hop when they chose this option. The RFU decided to instigate a one-year moratorium to allow the magnitude of the move to sink in, but other unions went straight into the new age. Needless to say, the Southern Hemisphere countries were in the lead as usual and had their players signed up by the individual unions very swiftly.

In England it was the clubs who began the process of contracting players, rather than the RFU, and wealthy businessmen came into the sport as owners. Both events still form the central issues facing our game and, despite calls from all sides for peace to break out, the RFU and the leading clubs are still locked in discussion as to the best way forward for the game. In early 1998 we had the situation where Northampton, through their millionaire owner Keith Barwell, did not want any of their international players to tour in the summer. Keith Barwell was concerned about the amount of rugby those big-name players were facing. Clive Woodward, the England coach, had to make a difficult decision and it's one I would not wish on anyone. Clive needed to know that every player taking part in the Five Nations championship would be available to tour in the Southern Hemisphere in the summer. If the answer was no, Clive had every right to leave those players out of the Five Nations squad. It was hard to believe, but we were in danger of denying a player the right to turn out for his country and, thankfully, Northampton relented and common sense prevailed. Both sides in the argument had valid points and they need to be addressed sooner rather than later because the 1999 World Cup in Wales is fast approaching.

Sir John Hall at Newcastle started the professional ball rolling in England and my club Wasps lost three high-profile players to the north-east revolution. Rob Andrew left us to become Newcastle's director of rugby, while Steve Bates and Dean Ryan became coach and captain respectively. That was a major shock to the Wasps system and the point when I took over the captaincy. It shook everyone up and suddenly the game realised that money really was going to be a significant factor in shaping our sport. Club loyalty had always been taken for granted and players stuck it out in the good times and the bad. Now the top players were being offered large salaries to uproot their families and link up with clubs they would never have considered joining before the game went professional.

This massive change in the game has not come about in peace and tranquillity, as players and supporters can testify. Thousands of column inches have been used up by rugby writers desperately trying to chart the progress, or rather lack of progress, of the game's search for a happy professional future. The 1996–97 season was blighted by internecine warfare between the clubs and the RFU. It seemed that every week brought another area of conflict and, no matter what the players achieved on the pitch, it was overshadowed by the constant bickering and rows. Managing change is a fiendishly difficult task and I believe that both sides made mistakes. That was inevitable because the arrival of professionalism split the game.

The majority of the RFU's clubs, which total more than two thousand, stayed amateur and still remain that way today. That means the RFU is having to administer two games – the paid and the amateur – yet they are an amateur body themselves. This does not sit well with the top clubs, many of which are owned by wealthy businessmen, intent on applying their business experience to the game. Some clubs are overstretched financially and that has huge implications for players who are now full time. I feel for the guys at Bristol who have been deeply affected by their club's problems. Moseley also contracted players from all over the world and they uprooted themselves after receiving assurances of financial backing. Moseley and Coventry have agreed to sell their grounds to generate enough money to clear debts and pull once famous clubs back from the brink. How they got there is a matter for the game's leading officials to study and understand because, as with a team, you are only as strong as your weakest link. The clubs believe there are more than two thousand people in this country who rely on professional rugby for a living wage and we cannot afford to play fast and loose with their livelihoods.

The Southern Hemisphere countries are bemused by the problems we are creating in the North because they have made a smooth transition to professionalism. This is not surprising, given that their rugby was arguably more professional than many other paid sports even when it was operating in the amateur era! It is much simpler for New Zealand rugby because it is the most

England coach Clive Woodward was put in a terrible position by Northampton's threat not to release their players.

All Black rugby legend Zinzan Brooke, who is now playing and coaching in England with Harlequins.

important sport in that country and sponsors are always willing to get involved. In Britain, there are other established professional sports, like football, which makes it tougher for rugby union to attract attention and much-needed support. That is why it is absolutely vital we move forward in unity and free from the damaging rows that have featured in these early days of the professional game. The players and coaches are doing their bit to move the sport into the next century as a vibrant, exciting product and we need those key men who control the game off the pitch to follow suit. This is an exciting time for the game and we cannot afford to shoot ourselves in the foot.

If we could put the off-the-field problems to one side and concentrate purely on rugby, we could be unstoppable at international level. The constant warfare is an annoying distraction that gives a negative impression of the sport to the uncommitted and makes it that much harder to attract new supporters and investors. The longer the impasse continues the harder it will become to convince doubters that we have a sport that deserves to stand alongside the other great games of the world. Each World Cup has led to an increase in interest and playing numbers in the UK and leading international companies queue up to be part of this rugby bonanza. Clubs' attendances in the Allied Dunbar Premiership have been increasing at a marvellous rate, with Saracens reporting a forty per cent leap in 1998 compared with the previous year. They now play at a 22,000 seater stadium at Vicarage Road, also home to Watford FC. It's just a couple of years since Wasps took the pitch against Saracens at their old home in Southgate where a couple of thousand fans stood around on a muddy council-owned park with rope strung from wooden stakes marking out the area of the ground. My own club, Wasps, has swapped homely Sudbury, with its tiny stand, for the hi-tech and all-seater surroundings of Loftus Road and we love the new home. The game is ready to lift off into a new era of success – if the RFU and the clubs can find a way to press the launch button together.

# 8
# Playing
# for England

## Letter in the post

I have kept most of the personal correspondence from the Rugby Football Union because to me, they signify important moments in my life. Some of the letters are good, others bad and some indifferent. The happiest are the ones telling me of selection for the next England game. I treasure the first letter that told me of my selection for the squad to play South Africa at Twickenham in 1995, the match which saw me win a first cap as a replacement. Then, there is the letter informing me of selection to start a match for the first time, against Western Samoa. I cannot throw away that kind of memento. No doubt some players do treat these letters as just another piece of paper, instructions to be followed and binned afterwards. But that's not me.

Every game for England is a unique occasion in terms of personal history and the history of the national team. As a rugby player you are privileged to be given the opportunity to represent your country and it's important to recognise the huge significance of the moment. Equally, it is important that those notifying you do it in the correct way, which hasn't always been the case. There is the classic story of Mark Rose, a member of my own club Wasps, who had made it into the England B team at the same time that Marcus Rose, the Harlequins full back, was in the senior England team. You don't have to be a genius to see the confusion that could reign in that kind of situation. Mark, the flanker, was selected to play for England B but, for some reason known only to Mark, he told the RFU it would better for him to help his mum move house that weekend rather than play for England B. Some weeks later, after his mum had moved house, Mark got another letter from the RFU saying that he had been selected for the full England team. No doubt he was rather surprised about this and rang the RFU to say how delighted he was to be given this chance, only to be told by the people at the RFU that a mistake had been made and the letter should have been sent to Marcus Rose, the England full back, instead.

I learnt of my selection for one game while driving along listening to the radio on my way to an England training session. That kind of story is repeated by many members of the England squad over recent years. The media are so hot on the trail of who is in the side and who is not that confidential, or what the public assumes is confidential, information leaks out. I don't know how the media manage it, but they get to deliver the news before the postman. It must have been dreadful to discover you had been left out of the side through the wrong channels, but that shouldn't occur in the future, particularly not under the current management team. The letter from Clive Woodward is now formal confirmation that you have made it and I compare it to discovering how much money you actually have, or don't have, in the bank. You only realise the truth when looking at a statement in your hand!

The RFU letter offers congratulations and tells you that you have won a place in the squad for the next game and the chance to bid for a position in the team. It's on headed notepaper and these days the letter is signed off by Clive which is a significant change. It used to be an RFU official whose name appeared at the bottom of the letter but now the coach informs his players and that's only right. It's an integral part of the whole England squad process and the way the game has evolved. The coach will also try and make a telephone call to reach a particular player if he has been dropped or brought in for the first time to ensure he does not hear the news from a third party. It's a courteous way of behaving.

# Slow build-up

The notification letter contains a date and a time for the squad to assemble and this could be the Saturday night or during the Sunday of the weekend before the international. Players turn up at different times at a hotel in Richmond, our base for home games at Twickenham. With the introduction of Sunday rugby, not everyone is available to come to the hotel on Saturday evening and there has to be some flexibility. There needs to be an unwinding process for those players involved in games at the weekend and that means Sunday is very relaxed and low key. A feeling of knitting together with everyone under one roof continues until Monday night. By taking this route we are ensuring that the squad is in the best possible frame of mind for what will be a very hard week-long mental and physical challenge.

International rugby is a very draining mental exercise and that is why countries, including New Zealand, are trying to cut down the number of test matches they ask their players to undertake in a twelve-month period. We don't want to saturate the market place with too many matches and we also need to cut down the strain on the players taking part.

When each player arrives he is allocated a room either of his own or sharing with another squad member. Previous squads always shared rooms and that meant you could end up with the roomy from hell, someone like Jeff Probyn, the Wasps prop, who loved to turn on every electrical item. His room-mates would wake up in the middle of the night to find Jeff watching the Baby Muppets just for something to do. The worrying aspect of this was he knew all the Muppet names! He also had the irritating habit of making a sound like a telephone that had you reaching for the handset at all hours, only to discover no one at the other end. Other players were snorers, or you could be in a situation after training where you fancied just a chicken sandwich and a pot of tea and your roomy was only interested in downing endless steak sandwiches.

Before they gave players their own rooms there used to be a belief that a 'roomist' policy was operated by the selectors. Sadly, it often was the case and you could work out if you were going to play by checking the name alongside yours on the hotel register. If you were a front-row player and found out your room-mate was the current hooker, it was almost certain to be a happy week with a place in the side.

We shared rooms on the Lions tour to South Africa and that helped create a special atmosphere and spirit. The tour started with eighteen England players on the room list and parochialism could have caused a problem. However, it was worked in such a way that two English guys never stayed together. We all moved around and that helped to break down barriers, which can exist for some time because some players are good at mixing while others find it hard as it's not in their nature.

The most important aspect of the England week at Richmond is that we must be able to prepare as thoroughly as possible. You never want to be in the position of making the excuse, 'Well, we didn't have enough time to get ready.' In years gone by, England would meet on the Friday night and play on Saturday afternoon at Twickenham. Those days have gone forever.

Even in the latter days of amateur rugby, England were striving to be as professional as possible and they started meeting on Wednesdays, but that was difficult for many players. They had jobs that needed their full attention and taking time off for every match was an added pressure to deal with. Now you have to be so thorough in the assessment of your own team, as well as the opposition, that it's important to put players in the right environment with enough time to deal with all the aspects of the preparation. The slow start to the week is welcomed by the players because it allows everyone to begin focusing on the job in hand with the ultimate aim of peaking at 3 p.m. on the following Saturday.

# A start not an end

The place where we meet up is both relevant and irrelevant because you want to create an environment to make England successful, not one that makes the players feel comfortable. We don't want players turning up at a very good hotel and thinking, 'This is great, now I can relax!' It must be very clear that by winning selection for England, a player hasn't reached the end of the road; it's actually the start of a whole new rugby challenge. A door has opened for that player and when he walks through it, the challenge he faces is bigger than anything he has ever tackled. Some players never grasp the opportunity that being selected for England offers and are content just to have made the team. Being selected for England is a recognition of your rugby talents but it should also be a chance for each player to take those talents to a higher level and, at the same time, become something special as a person. Anyone who turns up believing they have gained admission to a holiday home and will get the chance to swan around, has fatally misunderstood the situation and won't stay in the squad.

When the England team assembles at the start of an international week, it's a coming together of the élite. These are the best rugby players in England and it should be viewed that way and players must arrive knowing that at the end of the week they must run out and represent their nation and carry the hopes and desires of millions of people. That's something that must never be taken for granted. I am not saying there's not time for fun and relaxation but we can never lose sight of why we are all together in this one place at this particular time in our rugby careers.

The whole week operates under a schedule that the coaching team has put together but we are not as regimented under this management. You have to be flexible because the challenges you face are different in every game. The venue is different and the kick-off time can be earlier than normal, which has a knock-on effect. You have flexibility on the playing side and an opportunity to pick new players to give England the best chance of winning. Training may be switched from afternoon to morning and then reversed the following day, while dealing with bad weather is another factor that has to be taken into consideration. The coaches are accountable and responsible for setting out the week's training schedule and their job is to create an environment which allows the players to be successful. This is done in consultation with the captain and senior players. The coaches have authority to set the parameters by which the team lives during that week but these should be used only as guidelines.

The current management team has ensured, quite rightly, that when we do train, the squad is given the best available facilities. This is England and you would expect the squad to be given the best because we have left behind the club arena and what's good enough at that level. Given the help the squad receives, it is natural to expect a great performance in every match but there are no guarantees in life; you can only do everything humanly possible to give the team the best chance of triumphing.

# Teams within teams

During the week, the teams within the team evolve and hold their own meetings when we are away from the training ground. We are a very united squad and no matter what role you hold as a player, coach or member of the support staff, you have a part to play in the 'team'. In the team meetings you talk about what is being planned for the week in terms of training, what medical treatment is available and the type of relaxation opportunities, such as visiting the cinema. Ultimately, the coaches are responsible for organising the team meetings and ensuring that they get across all the information they feel is relevant for the particular opposition we are facing. In a rugby team, there is the front row, second row, back row, half backs, midfield and back three, all of whom form their own 'teams' and hold their own meetings, although who knows what the front row are talking about when they get together!

It's important to work as units in a team and when you come together the information and ideas from the different units melt down into one big pool which we can all draw from. That's a fundamental aspect of the week and I like to keep the meetings as short as possible so that we don't get bogged down. There are certain basics that everyone must be aware of, such as the strengths and weaknesses of the opposition and how we are going to play.

You can talk about expectation and the mental and physical challenges but, ultimately, the players have to deliver the goods. In the past, there has been a problem with too much talking and there's no doubt in my mind that a balance has to be found. There are so many resources available to the squad that we should never be in a position of not having the relevant piece of equipment or information. If there is something that can help make the difference between winning and losing, there can be no excuse for not utilising it during the week.

Video analysis forms an important part of the team meeting and this focuses not only on the opposition but on the strengths and weaknesses of our own recent performances. We have experts who watch the opposition, build up dossiers and compile statistical information from which they predict what could happen in certain circumstances. For instance, it may be that an opposition team mainly kicks high for the backs to chase when they have a line out on their own 10 metre line. But remember this is only a guideline, you have to be prepared to expect the unexpected, especially at test level. You can look at the England team as a business and the staff involved all have different attributes that, when utilised properly, make a significant difference. For example, some people are good at information-gathering, while others specialise in presenting that information in a coherent and interesting way. Others can digest that presentation and formulate a new strategy, one that best suits the team as it goes into a particular international. It's a bit like a Formula One racing team where the success of the whole operation depends on each person doing their job properly. You may only be the guy deputed to wipe the driver's visor, but if you mess up you put everything in jeopardy. The job of the coaching staff is to reduce all that in-put into a form that will best help us win the game. We can use overhead projectors, blackboards and flip charts, plus the video units, but they all lead to the reality of the training pitch where we must put these new strategies into effect. Hopefully, everything that has been digested in those team meetings will have become second nature for the players both in training and in the game.

Yes, there is a lot to take in over the week but individuals don't get picked at this level if they do not have the capacity to absorb the relevant information and use it on the field at the right time. You have to learn a lot in a short time and operate at a frantic pace, but that is international rugby. It's why we love to play at this level and gain the intense enjoyment of reaping the fruits of all the hours in the team rooms and on the training pitch. For me, you cannot beat that satisfaction.

Rugby should be a simple game and while it is great to have all those support staff compiling important facts, unless everyone in the team can understand what you are aiming to achieve, it's wasted. People should not get blinded by the science of the game and we try to ensure that doesn't happen within the squad. You have to retain an ability to be adaptable and flexible because opponents are doing the same analytical job on you and they work out counter-measures. You have to evolve and improve all the time to stay one step ahead of the opposition. If you haven't read *The Art of War* by Sun Tzu, then read it and you'll understand what I mean.

# And relax

Lightening the atmosphere is important and without making players sound like robots, you have to be able to switch on and off during the week. There are times when you have to work extremely hard but, you must also enjoy the rest periods. For your own sanity, you have to shut off the brain and just chill out for a little while. It's this ability to switch on and off that separates the good players from the great ones. Different players relax in different ways. You can

Austin Healey – one of the new England card-pool sharks.

guarantee a card school will be going on somewhere in the hotel during the evening once the business side of the day has been completed. In the past new boys were picked off by the old hands such as Dean Richards, Mike Teague and Peter Winterbottom. They were fantastic guys and great to get on with, but you entered their web of cards at your peril.

There are other forms or relaxation, including golf. When we have a rest period I crash out and hit the bed or just talk with other members of the squad. It's not often that you all get together and it's an opportunity to talk shop; if you cannot learn something from the best players in England, who can you learn from? There would have to be a serious communication problem within the squad if this atmosphere could not be created.

Every day you spend together strengthens the vital bond that must always be there in any great team. I am not a big television-watcher, except for sport which I am bonkers about; I prefer learning in other ways. The great thing about rugby, and the tours in particular, is that you get to soak up so much foreign culture. I try to get out and about in Wales, Scotland, Ireland and France when we play there during the Five Nations. Those are opportunities that should not be missed. You are what you are exposed to in life and if you take in more than the four walls of your hotel you are going to reap a tangible benefit.

When you spend an entire week together, it's important also to take time to be your own man. Some players prefer this way of operating, while others want to be in the middle of what is going on all the time. I find it's best to get into your own routine and not let anything or anyone upset that system. People respond in different ways and I have been involved in teams where players are laughing and joking an hour before the game but come kick-off time, they are totally focused. I look at the 100 metres Olympic final and see someone like Linford Christie ten minutes before the gun and recognise the same kind of focus. Christie is only thinking about that stretch of track and doesn't take any notice of the antics of the American runners who are joking and talking alongside him, trying to wind him up. In a rugby team, you get a sense of how a player wants to prepare, whether he wants to talk or remain silent because he is in the right mental tunnel.

# The final run-in

The coaches have to recognise when the players are reaching this point in the week and must prepare to hand over the team to the captain and the senior guys for that final run-in to the match. They have created the right atmosphere, given the players all the relevant information during the week and then, normally towards the latter half of the week, they step back. The coach recognises the moment when he could be accused of doing too much and it's time for the players to take ownership of the team and responsibility for the match. They are the only ones who play in the game.

# Match day

On match day, you have breakfast when you feel like it. Some players like a lie-in but, having a young daughter, I am used to early starts and eating lunch at the sort of time others are having their morning meal. I cannot hang around in bed once I have woken up and I get dressed and start to focus in on the game. I used to do a paper round and maybe that's why I still get up so early. One thing the round taught me is that Londoners read a lot of papers in the morning!

People have different dietary needs and with all the advice we now get about nutrition, you can work out a programme of food that will ensure you reach kick off fed and hydrated in the right way and feeling ready to give your best. I don't have a problem about watching calories because I don't put on much weight at this stage of my life, while some players do have that problem. I am a firm believer that if you are calm in body and mind, it will help you prepare for the game. During the match there will be opportunities to do what you feel is best, but if you do what someone tells you at breakfast, that gets you into a mind set for doing what you are told and you stop thinking for yourself. Deciding what to have at breakfast may not sound like a major moment during a match day, but it starts the vital decision-making process off. It's the way I start to get my head around the day anyway, and I don't always have the same breakfast – keeping my options open.

If you look at those sportsmen who are at the peak of their powers there is always a ritualistic routine they follow. In tennis, Pete Sampras bounces the ball exactly the same number of times before each serve, wipes away sweat with the same arm and sweat band and then fires off the serve. It's a ritual that he finds puts him in the right frame of mind to win the point and, ultimately, the match. Golfers have the same twitches before hitting the drive. The idea is to get into the groove and focus on a mental tunnel that is successful for you. I have my own way of preparing on match days and the same can be said of other members of the squad who will always do their laces up in a certain way or have strapping put on certain areas of their body. If that routine has made them good players, it will also help make them even better ones.

The coach journey to Twickenham from the hotel is a wonderful experience because it's the culmination of the whole week and everyone gets a real sense of occasion. You are on your way to something special and the coach tends to be quiet with players listening to Walkmans or just staring out at the crowds that have started to make their way to the ground. Some players insist on sitting in exactly the same seat in the coach and hang their coats up in a particular way and then it's a time for reflection and collecting your thoughts. I don't mind music being played for everyone on the coach, or even in the dressing room, because it stimulates my preparation. Once you get off that coach, things are never the same again; you walk into a marvellous arena. I often think that journey and the moment when we rise to leave the coach are like a parachute brigade flying out on a mission. The red light comes on and, when the green light shows, you jump.

# In the dressing room

The dressing-room atmosphere is difficult to put across in black and white; in fact, it is indescribable. So much is going on and players are zoned into their own particular preparations. The medical staff are strapping some players up, while others are walking around, not saying anything, putting on their kit. We go out on to the pitch for the official photograph, have a further chat to the referee and try to get a feel for what's coming. Everything is positive and the coaches will be there, pushing and prodding you mentally to key into the important aspects of the game and what needs to be done in the coming eighty minutes of rugby.

Once the referee has come into the dressing room to check the boots and the padding we are wearing, it really starts to get intense and we have one of the back-room staff shouting out the time left before we have to enter the tunnel and run out into that crescendo of noise. The key element in that period is to ensure that, having built up to such an intensity, you maintain it for the whole match and don't let it dissipate after running on to the pitch and singing the national anthems.

# Let's go!

It's an incredible feeling, seeing the dressing-room door open and hearing someone shouting 'Let's go!' Then it really is time to put all the training and preparation into practice. It all has to come out at that very moment and you maintain that edge by treating each game as if it is your last. If you could bottle that feeling up and sell it, it would be the rarest commodity around and no price would be enough to buy it. I am a firm believer that everyone is good at something, it's just that many people don't get the chance to find out what they have within themselves and express it in the right way. I have found what I enjoy and hopefully what I am good at and it's a wonderful thing to experience. Winning does mean everything but to appreciate the best you must have experienced the worst, otherwise you can never fully understand what you have achieved. There are games of rugby that you lose and they live with you for the rest of your sporting life. Paris in 1998 is one that will be with me and I am sure that the 1995 World Cup final defeat will never be erased from the memories of the All Blacks. They will take that defeat to their graves and the loss to England in 1993 is another  that will haunt them. The same goes for English players who lost to Scotland in 1990 and the World Cup final a year later to Australia.

Once you do appreciate the massive difference between winning and losing at the highest sporting level, you can fully understand what you have achieved when you win an international rugby match. It's easy to find something positive from the wins in your career, but I have also learnt something from every game I have lost.  The painful lessons should ensure that you work that much harder, never to feel like that again. You never stop learning.

# And after

It does take time to come down from the high that is an international rugby match, both in physical and mental terms. If I lose a game I take it very personally and I don't exorcise that ghost until the next match. But I try and be positive about the mistakes that were made and commit myself to not making them again. The game is never forgotten; it goes into the memory bank to be drawn on at some point in the future. That's what makes experienced players so vital to any team and gives them an edge.

I believe in creating élitism. If you are good enough you are in but you drop out if you are not. When you are picked for England you should feel that you are part of something very special and that should never leave you. If you achieve that goal, you can create something that becomes unstoppable and, ultimately, unbeatable.

# 9
# Captaincy

## Who should captain a rugby team?

The best man for the job is the obvious answer, although I believe the importance of the captain on the field at international level is not as crucial as those off the pitch assume. By that I mean the game is so fast and complicated these days that you must have decision-makers in key positions all over the team. It's impossible for one player to control everything that happens. The spine of the team – hooker, No. 8, scrum half and outside half – play a pivotal role and each of these players must be able to make tactical decisions in both attack and defence. As captain, you must ensure that the overall tactical plan is being applied, and maintain the team's channels of communication and focus at the various times when play stops.

Many people believe you cannot captain a team from the wing – too far from the action – or from hooker – head buried in the scrum. I don't agree and there have been successful club and international captains in both those positions. If a captain has players around him who accept the collective responsibility for taking decisions, any system can work. I play in the back row for my club and country but this does not mean I am going to be in a position to be able to call every move during eighty minutes. I rely on my half backs to put our game plan into operation and read play correctly as the match unfolds. The modern game demands a flexible approach and a clever mixture of running and tactical kicking. It is patently ridiculous for my outside half to look to me for the OK before kicking the ball each time! If he takes the wrong option I will make my views known straightaway, but I have to accept he felt that was the correct option at that time.

## Getting the message across

I believe the idea of the captain making a Henry V type speech to his troops in the dressing room is antiquated. I am still talking to my players in the final minute of injury time and that's a fact of modern rugby. I don't sit everyone down before we board the bus and give them a call to arms because, at this level, players have shown that mentally and physically they are capable of achieving a standard of rugby far higher than anyone else in their position. In the dressing room, there has to be a physical edge and mental hardness; there should be no need to shout and scream or bang your head against the wall. There needs to be an element of that, but it can often exist through the mere presence of the players. The captain has a message to get across and it is important to communicate clearly and positively. Staying composed is crucial to being successful.

There's one speech the captain can't side-step, however. I don't worry about getting on my feet at the post-match dinner until after the game is over. Then I just try to be myself because it will never come across in the right way if I try to be clever. In the post-match speech, you have to recognise the uniqueness of every international occasion and remember to thank both teams and the coaches, plus the referee and touch judges. They had a survey in America about what people feared most and death came second to public speaking, which neatly sums it up for me. I don't profess to be an expert and I don't have the knack I have seen in others. I just try to talk honestly, then it doesn't matter if people don't agree because I have been myself.

# Dealing with the media

The media are always searching for the ultimate 'piece' about a player and this can often lead to half-truths being reported as fact because they happen to fit the angle the writer is looking for in his story. I was told about the Italian sports reporter who got excited when England won the 1993 Rugby World Cup Sevens at Murrayfield when I was lucky enough to be part of the victorious team. This reporter spotted my Italian name and wanted to know more about my family to increase the length of his report for one of the papers in northern Italy. He kept on asking if my father was an Italian restaurant-owner because it fitted the stereotype he wanted. Eventually he discovered my father was, in fact, a former hotel manager but this did not have the same ring to it as reporting 'The son of an Italian restaurateur, who left home to offer Londoners classic dishes, has won the the World Cup.' In justification he informed the bemused British journalists, 'Well, the hotel had a restaurant, didn't it?' and proceeded to peddle the story about my father being an Italian chef made good in London.

In many ways, the captain's role has increased in importance off the field in the last decade. The sport is winning more space in newspapers and on radio and television and the captain and the team's leading players are the obvious focal point before and after matches. The Rugby Football Union has its own communications department which deals with all media enquiries and this acts

Captaincy – you need the support and help of your team to make it a success.

Top of the world, to the astonishment of so many! Winners of the World Cup Sevens, 1993.

My try in the World Cup Sevens final against Australia.

My back after a shoeing from Eastern Province.

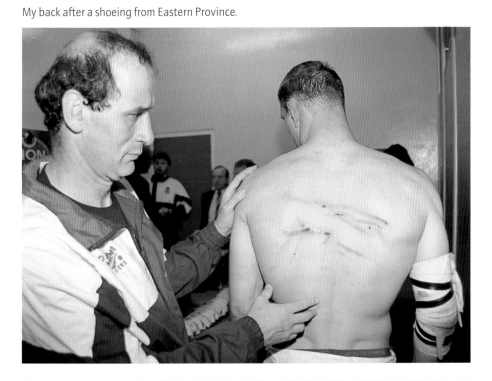

as a clearing house for interview requests. It can be very daunting to take your seat on the top table for a pre-match press conference and face banks of cameras and rows of journalists. Needless to say, the conferences are much easier to handle when the team is winning. The RFU communications department arranges seminars which are designed to equip every player with the tools needed to handle press and television interviews. Once you get into the swing of things it can become just another part of the pre-match build-up.

As captain, it appears that every television station in Europe wants a sound bite from me in the seven days before and after a test match and, of course, a lot of it is repetition. There are only a certain number of issues and questions that can be asked about them and I have to repeat the same answer on numerous occasions. How do I keep sounding interested? Well, you have to acknowledge that television, radio and newspapers reach millions of committed or potential rugby fans and we are in the market place. Rugby could not afford to buy the amount of advertising that is given for free in the week leading up to a big match and the old adage that any publicity is good publicity is often very true. Yes, there are times when you think 'Is this guy for real?' when a particularly dumb question is asked, but you have to take a deep breath, smile and try to give a reply which does not take the mick out of the reporter.

Many players write columns for newspapers and this is often achieved with the help of a reporter who is assigned to ghost the piece for you. It involves speaking, either face to face or down the telephone, to a writer who then puts your ramblings into a form that appears to make you a wordsmith. No doubt my old English teacher at Ampleforth wonders how L.B.N. Dallaglio can appear in the national newspapers each week! These columns do allow you a platform to explain points of view or talk about trends in the game. The Lions management banned anyone from writing a column during the 1997 tour to South Africa, as they felt they could become a source of disunity. I can see their point, although many readers would argue that players' columns are more likely to put you to sleep than incite rioting in the streets!

As with other sports, I believe it's important to have a code of conduct to cover statements in the media. Rugby is an intensely physical game that needs to avoid personal conflicts generated by derogatory comments made in the press. This is particularly important in the build-up to internationals because, quite naturally, writers are looking for the best scoop. Their sports desks are always going to give more space to a piece suggesting a game is going to explode rather than a story predicting peace and tranquillity.

Brian Moore, the former England hooker, was very clever at using the media in the days before a game with France. His most famous comment, clearly designed to wind up the opposition, was, 'Playing France is like facing fifteen Eric Cantonas: brilliant but brutal.' Not surprisingly, the French were outraged but Mooro had achieved his aim and once again England won the psychological battle as well as the match. England have used comments from opponents to help psyche the team up just before taking the pitch and I know of occasions when an inflammatory story has been pinned on the dressing-room wall to act as a trigger. To date, I am unaware of any of the Dallaglio columns being treated in this way, and they are more likely to be keeping cod and chips warm rather than stirring up anger in the Celtic nations.

# The celebrity game

The England rugby union captain, as Will Carling discovered, has a new status in British sport and can find himself on the news as well as the sports pages. Celebrity is not a problem previous England captains had to deal with. Being appointed captain of your country is the greatest honour but you don't really understand how it will change your life until it happens. The smallest detail of your private life becomes of interest to feature writers for newspapers and magazines and the sheer demand for your time gets wearing. That is where Ashley Woolfe, my manager, comes into his own. He is able to help organise the off-the-field commitments that fit in around my life as a professional rugby player. It would be impossible for me to attempt to handle everything without help, and my rugby would suffer. I often wonder how those players who helped raise the profile of the England team and the game as a whole in the 1980s, managed to juggle their rugby and a full-time job.

I have a young family and ensuring that a part of my life remains private is important. As a professional rugby player I acknowledge the need to promote the game and help its profile, but where do you draw the line? It's a question that will not go away as long as the game keeps grabbing the headlines and continues to give rugby players a celebrity status of sorts.

The rugby public is as mad about the game as the players and our sport triggers constant debate and club-house discussion. As captain you become the embodiment of the side, in the good times and bad, and the paying rugby public are always ready to offer advice! The kind of attention I am now attracting is nothing new to people from other sports but that doesn't make it any easier to deal with. In the past, the RFU would just let a captain muddle through and he had to learn on the hoof, but times have changed, even if the downside of the honour of leading your country has not.

I was, so I discovered after the match, called Judas by some fans at Saracens in March 1998 and this was the direct result of what I have talked about. The on-going argument between the clubs and the RFU involving contracts had reached the papers and reports appeared claiming I was about to sign a deal with the RFU. This was both untrue and irritating because I am totally committed to both Wasps and England. I opted to keep quiet; in those

The family – a proud father gatecrashes a lovely picture of Alice and baby Ella.

circumstances you cannot win. Any comment about a false report will give it some kind of credence and I was not prepared to do that, even if it meant I had to accept those taunts. Every professional player has options when it comes to contracts and I am still contracted to Wasps who want to take up a year's option for 1998–99. I signed a contract with England, which all the squad players did, before the pre-Christmas internationals and it included the summer tour to the Southern Hemisphere.

# 10
# Delivering the goods

## The team behind the team

Rugby fans probably don't appreciate just how much back-up players receive today. When we toured South Africa with the Lions in 1997 a truck was needed for all the training kit and this also pulled the hi-tech scrummage machine that was to become a mobile instrument of torture! Besides being provided with a whole wardrobe of kit designed specifically for training, the Lions players also received leisure gear and clothing for official functions. It all had to be carried around South Africa and I hate to think what kind of excess baggage bill we ran up.

The training aids ranged from that scrummage machine to boxing equipment, chest armour for use during tackle sessions, tackle bags and pads, plus other specialist aids that helped recreate as many match situations as possible. When we had finished with all of that stuff for the day, we would often assemble in the team room to watch video clips of our own play and for an appreciation of the opposition.

The Lions players received individual videos which showed only what each of us had done in a game and these were very illuminating. You have an idea in your own mind about how the game went on a personal level, but the actuality can be a bit of a shock. No matter how far away from the prying eyes of the video camera you thought you were when that pass was knocked on, it's there for everyone to see.

It's natural for everyone to concentrate on what happens on the rugby pitch for those eighty minute, plus whatever injury time the referee adds on. However, the match is merely a culmination of a week-long build-up that takes place on training pitches and in team rooms with the use of a multitude of aids that are helping propel the game into the twenty-first century. In the so-called good old days, teams trained twice a week at night with plenty of shuttle runs and various scrummage and line-out sessions, while the nancy-boy backs messed around with the one training ball they were allowed from restricted club funds. Rugby's giant leap forward, instigated by professionalism, has built on changes that the more enlightened clubs, players and coaches had already started to bring into the game. At Wasps we have an extensive back-up team to support the players and it covers every possible area of the game.

When professional rugby teams take the training pitch, it is to follow a set routine that has been chosen by the coach, even if it may appear that we are making it up as we go along. Each session has defined goals and there is nothing more satisfying than working on an aspect of the game in training and then seeing it come off in a match situation. At least it convinces the coach we really were listening!

# Fitness work

Fitness is like a pyramid and to reach a peak at various times during the season you must have built a wide base. That is achieved in the pre-season period after at least a four-week break from all rugby. It's vital to have a period when you are completely switched off from the sport and that can be difficult when summer tours are part of the schedule.

After the rest period, you start with strength work, using weights under a programme set up by the club in June, July and August. Endurance becomes a factor around the same time; like the weights work, it goes into the bank to be drawn out later. For example, the endurance work can involve 8x150 metre runs or 20x200 metre runs on various days.

At Ampleforth we used to follow a system that started with a 100 metre run, 30 seconds off, a 200 metre run, rest, then 400 metres, then 200 metres and finally 100 metres. This was repeated three times and I found it an extremely good exercise for building up fitness.

You are not trying to break world records, just to maintain the quality of your work, and the stopwatch never lies. Keeping up with your previous times, or bettering them, gives an indication of how the fitness work is really going.

Many players use heart-rate monitors because you have to know that you have worked at a level that will bring real benefit and make you fitter. Once the pyramid is built, you should check your fitness level every eight weeks to ensure you have a measurement to work from. Variety is the key; you cannot endlessly go through the same routine in the weights room or on the pitch and, furthermore, at various times, you need to sharpen everything up to prepare for matches.

Nowadays, we are more aware of the need for rest periods and that is why professional advice is important because it's vital to get the balance right. You can use a rugby ball in the fitness routines but you shouldn't be obsessed about carrying the ball all the time.

# Injury treatment

Along with all the fitness advice, technical back-up, kit and specialised training aids, there is another area of the game that has come on in leaps and bounds in recent years. It is the prevention, treatment and recovery from injury. The days when a bucket and sponge, liberally doused in freezing cold water, constituted state-of-the-art medical support have, thankfully, been consigned to the history books – well, at least at Wasps they have! I always believed that the application of the cold sponge did more to convince a player he did not need another shock like that to his system than anything to do with its mystical healing properties. After all, medical research has yet to identify exactly what special restorative powers a mucky sponge and dodgy water actually possess. Now clubs like Wasps have extensive medical support and cold water and sponges are restricted to car-washing duties in the club car park.

We are professional players and it's only natural that a club like Wasps would want to treat us like assets. They have invested large sums of money and considerable time and effort in our careers and injury is the major worry for anyone involved in the game. I cannot stress strongly enough just how important it is to have trained phsyiotherapists and sports injury doctors attached to the club. Not only does this allow quick and expert diagnosis but a player gets vital information on how he can best help heal the injury. Touch wood I have stayed clear of serious injury in my career and sensible precautions, such as stretching before, during and after exercise and sticking to a training and nutritional regime devised for me by the club's experts, have been crucial.

# Padding

I realise that the arrival of what some people consider to be illegal padding and the use of body armour is causing concern. I don't believe it signals the start of a road that eventually leads to rugby becoming as dependent on padding and protecive gear as American football. It is being regulated and I can't see a problem if everyone takes the sensible approach to this subject.

It would not be unfair to say that the tackles we see these days are bigger than before in the game. Four or five years ago, when I started at senior level, the hits were not as physically demanding. That has a lot to do with professionalism, with players being on specific diets and benefiting from personalised

Training with the England squad at Bisham Abbey.

weight-training regimes which make them bigger and heavier in terms of sheer muscle bulk. Year after year, players are getting faster and bigger and that's a natural progression for the game. The ball is in play a lot longer, therefore more tackles are being made. Padding is a natural consequence because these precautions safeguard the body. It's a sensible move. It's like wearing a seat belt in a car. I am comfortable about wearing shoulder padding.

# Eating for success

At Wasps we have been given considerable help in sorting out what to eat and what to avoid; the same kind of advice is offered at England level and, of course, many of the ideas are pretty obvious – even to the front-row guys!

Here are some of the Do's and Don'ts that I follow:

1. Choose foods that are baked, grilled or steamed rather than fried or cooked in oil.
2. Choose rice, pasta or potatoes as the main component of your meal. Ask for extra bread with all meals.

3. Include plenty of vegetables or salad.
4. Ask for dressings and sauces on the side and add just a small amount. Request that foods are cooked in little or no oil.
5. Choose tomato-based sauces instead of cream-based ones.
6. Drink alcohol in moderation. Order water with your meal.

If I go to an Italian restaurant I will opt for pasta with tomato, or grilled chicken, rather than cheese-topped pizza, or pasta with cream and butter sauce. You can still have a great night out, so just watch those ingredients and if you do transgress, make sure no one can see you!

# Off the sauce

I still get people coming up and asking about the drinking sessions, the singing of dirty rugby songs and general mayhem associated with rugby. Now I don't claim to be teetotal but if anyone thinks he can, as Mickey Skinner would say, 'Go on the lash, fatboy' and still train the next day, he has a unique constitution or a death wish. You cannot afford, as a professional athlete, to treat your body like that. In the amateur days some players did like a couple of beers the night before a game, but that was then. Even the most stubborn front-row forward has

Jeff Probyn (left) and Paul Judge Rendall prove that wine, women and beer can still be part of the game.

been won over by the enormous amount of evidence produced by our nutritional and medical support staff which shows how debilitating alcohol is to an athlete's body. I am not saying we celebrate an international win with water and orange juice, it's just that the build-up to the game no longer includes the odd visit to the pub. It's not even a case of the management having to lay down the law because being a professional requires total commitment from each player. You are messing around with your body and your career prospects and everyone knows that one bad game can cost you and your team-mates the chance of winning. If that performance could be traced back to a heavy night on the sauce, the player could be justly accused of unprofessional behaviour. No one should let their team-mates down.

This probably gives the impression of a game shorn of its characters and wild nights. Nothing could be farther from the truth. Rugby will always retain its sense of fun, no matter how heavy the demands of professionalism become. There is another worry that those coming into the game will arrive with rugby as a career option rather than a passion. That's why it is vital that we do not lose sight of what made this game so successful and still keeps the majority of players in England turning out every week for their amateur sides. Those guys play for the sheer love of the sport, for the beers in the bar after the game and the chicken vindaloo challenge at the local Indian at midnight. Do I miss that? I don't believe I have given up that kind of camaraderie and, to be honest, I am not a great fan of vindaloo!

# The rugby family, alive and well

It's vital for the future of the game that we cater for all levels and people must be allowed to find the intensity of rugby that they are comfortable with. Players must be allowed to move up, others will want to move down the ladder. An open door is critical. Young players who believe they have what it takes to be a professional should be able to dip their toes in the water and make up their minds. Similarly, there are ambitious junior clubs who want to be part of the professional game but finance governs just what kind of a showing they can make.

One of the great challenges facing rugby at the highest level is to retain a sense of perspective, to keep contact with the supporters who are a key element in any professional sport and to remember they love the game as much as we do. However, they now pay a lot more to come and watch us perform and included, I hope, in the growing number of supporters at club matches are fans new to the game. The increased admission price will give those fans the right to voice their dissatisfaction if the product on offer is not good enough. Club rugby used to be a bit of a joke in England but then along came the leagues and the fast track to professionalism was discovered.

# Bums on seats

It's only right to talk about the game as product because we are in a very competitive market place. There is only a finite number of punters out there and they have the ultimate say in where their hard-earned cash is spent. Unless we offer them a game to excite and enthrall, much-needed spectators will head off to other sports.

I love going to watch Chelsea when my rugby commitments allow, and it's an expensive exercise with no guarantee of satisfaction (although any kind of win over Man United is worth taking!). Rugby has enjoyed a period of acclimatisation but the honeymoon is over. Rugby union has reached a hiatus and the decisions taken over the next twelve months will reshape the game forever. The paying public want value for money and the challenge we have to meet is to give it to them, week in, week out, or the sport I love will wither. We have the support of Chris Wright, the owner of Loftus Road PLC (the company that has Wasps and QPR under its umbrella) and thanks to men like him the game has received millions of pounds of investment. It would be a terrible waste if, by our own actions, we failed to give the public the right kind of product. After all, the development costs have been enormous.

At England level we have a whole range of support staff to look after every need. Some may call it pampering. A glance through an international match programme offers a list of those men and women who make up the back-room staff. They range from a baggage man to a sports psychologist and we are only now catching up with and moving ahead of other countries who have used this kind of specialist support for years. There is nothing wrong with sampling concepts and ideas from other sports and we should always be open to new ideas and systems. There is obviously a balance to be found between playing and resting and rugby is trying to come to terms with this conundrum.

As a sport becomes more successful, its marketing people want to cash in. Those of us lucky enough to play at international level have that added demand and pressure on our time. It's one of the hottest issues in the game today and one that has to be addressed by players, coaches and officials. I want to play this game for as long as possible and that will require a sensible playing programme, sensible goals that I set myself and a sensible structure to accommodate club and international rugby.

# 11
# Rugby round the world

Once you have assembled a team of talented individuals and found the right coaching panel, the next step is to decide on a style of play that will bring the best out of everyone; that is, once you have pointed out that it's not possible to go straight on tour, no matter what kind of remarkable deal the treasurer has conned out of Mrs Miggin's Guest House in Redruth! At international level many people believe that the Southern Hemisphere sets the agenda and the rest of the world follows. I don't believe that is true, and England are certainly not going down on bended knee to anyone; we are determined to set out our own stall. Looking around the world of rugby, there are certain basic elements that go into the make-up of each leading nation and here is my verdict on those major teams and what I believe makes them so difficult to play.

## New Zealand

What sets New Zealand apart from other rugby nations is their ability to react faster than any other team to a given situation on the pitch. They went 21 points down to England in November 1997 and came back to draw the match. They were 26 points down to South Africa in Johannesburg the previous year and still found a way of battling back into a match that most people had already written off as a Springbok triumph. This priceless ability to make decisions under the most intense pressure allows the All Blacks to win games other sides would lose.

It is a truism to say rugby is the New Zealand religion and to pull on the All Black jersey is to join an exclusive club the lineage of which stretches back to the start of this century. Every young rugby player in New Zealand has his or her eyes focused on the ultimate goal and that breeds a special rugby culture. Throw in the physical power of the Maori section of the community and a regular influx of Islanders from Western Samoa, Fiji and Tonga, and you have a heady mix that becomes almost unstoppable when guided on to the pitch by a coach of John Hart's undoubted class. The All Blacks have been world leaders for a long time and even when they haven't been rated number one, they have been pretty close and always trying to make changes that would allow a return to the pinnacle of the game.

South Africa will argue that they are the best in the world at the moment, due to their 1995 World Cup triumph, and what these two countries have in common is a desire to amend their domestic rugby in whatever way possible to help the national team triumph. It's an attitude we do not have in Britain and Ireland at the moment. All that matters to Kiwi and Springbok fans is that they can produce fifteen players who will rule the world and allow the entire country to bask in the reflected glory. New Zealand fans have been basking for a long time, thanks to the excellence of the current squad under Hart, and their domination has been almost complete since the 1995 World Cup final when they expected to beat the Boks and came unstuck. There were well-documented accusations of spiked tea and coffee leading to Kiwi players suffering on match day, but the history books will only record the final result to the Springboks.

The way the game is being played at the moment, any new law changes instigated by the International Rugby Board, who administer the game world

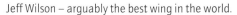
Jeff Wilson – arguably the best wing in the world.

wide, do come from the Southern Hemisphere. By the nature of the two halves of world rugby and their different seasons, the laws are often brought in in the South a good six months before they arrive with us. That gives those nations a head start and a priceless opportunity to work out just how revolutionary the changes will be and what measures must be taken to get the greatest benefit from them. It means we are often playing catch-up and, on that basis, England needs to get its act together with the IRB and start setting an agenda to suit us, instead of the Southern Hemisphere. Until we start beating the teams from the South on a regular basis, this power bloc is unlikely to be broken and their influence will continue to shape the game.

The game has changed dramatically in recent years following law changes and all the Southern Hemisphere teams, and New Zealand in particular, have recognised the need for power and pace with the ability to use these vital attributes explosively. Crossing the gain line at pace is critical and New Zealand's inclusion of Islanders and those with Maori ancestry gives them an edge because these men are naturally great athletes. New Zealand have established a structure below the national team level that will identify players of test potential and funnel them towards the All Blacks squad, and their system is second to none in achieving its stated aims.

A player can give himself the opportunity for a better life by excelling in rugby in New Zealand. There isn't a need to look abroad to play and that ensures the domestic competition is strong and maintains its strength year after year. English rugby must start developing from within, because that is the only way we will be able to go forward with the kind of strength in depth that makes it so difficult to beat the All Blacks at any stage of their season. In the past there was an almost slavish acceptance that the All Blacks were the ultimate rugby nation and whatever they did had to be followed, but you cannot accuse the current England set-up of that kind of attitude. At the same time you cannot help but admire the quality of rugby the All Blacks are producing against very different opposition at home and abroad over the last eighteen months. There is no doubt they are a great team, using every single player to create success.

We cannot replace our individuals with theirs. We have to accept that players like Christian Cullen, the full back, winger Jonah Lomu and No. 8 Zinzan Brooke are not found easily, but we do have our own strongmen and outstanding all-round performers who can express themselves successfully at international level.

The evidence of results and the volume of adulation that is heaped upon the All Blacks means they do have a mental edge over certain teams, but that makes the sense of achievement so much greater when you do manage to beat them – so I am told! The All Blacks are fired by a burning desire not to let their country down or the legion of players who have gone before them, running on to an international rugby pitch wearing the famous black jersey with the silver fern.

The Haka epitomises this ambition and let's be very clear, it is a war dance. Buck Shelford, in the 1980s, made it something very important. It is an attempt to win the psychological battle before the game has even started.

How you deal with it is down to the individual. David Campese and Michael Lynagh of Australia once kicked a ball to each other in the in-goal area while the All Blacks were doing the Haka.

I personally like and enjoy the Haka and tend to stare across at the opposition. Our hooker Richard Cockerill wants to get as close to the All Blacks as possible during the dance, but it is important to be respectful. Rugby is not war, but it's not that far away and the Haka lays down a challenge you must accept.

The competition created by New Zealand's domestic championship means that no one can stand around accumulating caps and even the biggest names, like Lomu, have been dropped for someone else who is in better form. It probably appeared incomprehensible to those outside New Zealand that they could consider going on to the pitch without a fully fit Lomu. But, there he was, reduced to the replacements bench because Glen Osborne was in better form. That is a powerful message to send out to the national squad and all those who want the chance to break into the All Blacks side. There is no comfort zone with the All Blacks and we are starting to achieve that situation with England.

I just cannot understand how we let a situation arise where England did not meet New Zealand for four years at a time. We were happy to continue beating Ireland, Wales, Scotland and occasionally, France. England was left to wallow in its own small world which made it that much harder to raise the playing standard when along came the Southern Hemisphere sides and the All Blacks in particular. In 1997, for the first time in our rugby history, England played New Zealand (twice), South Africa and Australia in consecutive tests and, although we did not manage a win, it was a tremendous learning experience for all those involved and something we will never forget.

As an England fan, I used to think that we had a great team in 1991 when the Grand Slam was won. That team went off to Australia and was hammered by 40 points. There are questions you must ask yourself in that situation. Do you want to be the best in Europe or on top of the world? The All Blacks have never had any difficulty answering that question and that is why they won the 1987 World Cup and will be amongst the favourites in 1999.

# South Africa

My perception of South Africa has been affected by the fact that they were missing from international sport for so long because of the sanctions imposed on the country while apartheid existed. I always used to think that New Zealand were by some way the best team in the world until 1992 when the Springboks were allowed back and managed to run the All Blacks very close in Johannesburg from a standing start. That was an awesome return and one that made the whole game sit up and take notice. The Springboks had somehow managed to maintain their standards, despite playing in a vacuum, and they have proceeded to get better and better with every year. This ability to return as a real power is testament to their commitment to rugby excellence and absolute belief that they can rule the rugby world, even though the majority of the country is football rather than rugby mad.

I was pleased not to have to make any political decisions about going to South Africa which is something England players faced in 1984. I went ten years later, fundamental changes to the lives of the majority had been made, and there was real excitement that England had turned up. The South Africans produce extremely gifted rugby players. I watched their youngsters playing in curtain-raiser matches before the England and later the Lions tour games and they were all in bare feet. All they wanted to do was run with the ball, keep it alive and play wonderful rugby. It was great to watch. You can see that if they are playing with such pace and using natural skills at that age, it's no wonder they turn into great players later in life at the highest level.

Their international style is different from New Zealand's and is born out of their long-held belief that forward power will win the day. They have always put emphasis on their play up front with a strong scrummage backed up by an astute kicking outside half. Defensively they are very committed to the tackle and organise themselves well, which makes it difficult to break them down, and allied to this is an attacking guile that is starting to be seen on a regular basis.

I have already mentioned the All Blacks' phenomenal ability to change the course of a game by switching tactics and an inability to do this used to be a weakness in the Springbok make-up. Because they have such an unshakeable belief that success will come if they continue to play through their massive forwards, it was hard for the Springboks to turn the course of a match that was not going their way. We saw that happening in the Lions tests in 1997 and other matches before that series, with the Springboks coming unstuck against a team that stood up to their forward onslaught. Under new coach, Nick Mallett, they have realised this is not the way to continue and are developing a style which is adaptable to every game. With their natural talent, they could become the first side successfully to defend the World Cup in 1999.

I know that the non-white community in South Africa is mainly interested in football but I saw the excitement generated when we went into the townships and took equipment for local players to use to play rugby. I accept that many of those visits were just photo-opportunities to increase the feel-good factor, but when you see how little they have, the joy that can be created through sport means everything. It would be good if South Africa could develop an integrated culture and white and black communities could take pride in the success of both their rugby and football teams on the world stage. It was obvious, even from the limited time I spent in the townships, that there are individuals with real talent and flair who need to be offered more than just one sporting option. If that talent is tapped, the Springboks could be an even greater challenge. God help us if they do get their act together.

# Australia

The Australians produce world-class players from a small base involving just three main states – Queensland, New South Wales and ACT (Australia Capital Territory). Rugby league and Aussie rules dominate the winter season in Australia, leaving the union game to fight for a share of the players who are on offer. You wonder how the Aussies can continually manage to produce a team that is truly competitive but it doesn't happen by chance. They have a very good structure in place that ensures the few good players around are identified and nurtured in the right environment to breed success. While on tour in Aus-

Tim Horan makes a break against New Zealand.

tralia, I visited their marvellous Institute of Sport which has fantastic facilities for a whole range of sports and covers every aspect of excellence. It's not by accident that Australia currently boasts the best cricket team in the world and that's a result of getting it right off the pitch.

They also concentrate on coaching and we see rugby league coaches making a real impact both inside and outside Australia which, apart from Bob Dwyer at Leicester, has yet to happen to the same extent in union. It's a fact that your team cannot become great on the world stage unless the structure and coaching is in place. The quality of the Australian play has improved enormously since they started playing New Zealand and South Africa on a regular basis. When New Zealand is so close, it really helps in creating a rivalry that spurs both countries on to try and put one over on the other. There is a healthy disrespect and that adds spice to the matches, particularly the Bledisloe Cup clashes that have produced some of the greatest games of rugby union I have ever watched.

The Australians are great at making you believe they run the ball all the time when, in truth, they are one of the most successful kicking outfits in the world. When you have players like Michael Lynagh and Nick Farr-Jones who can launch pin-point kicks and initiate an aerial bombardment, backed up by superb chasers like centres Tim Horan and Jason Little, you would be mad not to utilise them. There is no point having a strong kicking game if the rest of the team is not chasing correctly because all you are doing is giving the opposition free ball to run straight back at you. What I have noticed about the Wallabies is that they have their own unique playing style, and just concentrate on using the various skills within their own team. Everyone talks about the 1991 World Cup final when they defeated England and how they showed us running rugby throughout the tournament. They played that final very cleverly, using the boot to great effect.

The tri-nations tournament doesn't mean that familiarity between the All Blacks, Springboks and Wallabies breeds contempt; it allows each country to reach for the very top of the game. It becomes front-page news if one of the countries performs badly. But if the team is winning, everything else defers to the national cause. The sooner England realise that the better, because if we are to compete consistently and successfully the national good has to come first. If we continue as we are, a place amongst the second division of the game will be our level.

# France

The French are a law unto themselves and if they ever get their act together in terms of a real playing structure, they would overtake everyone in world rugby.

They have that massive capacity yet contrive to under-perform almost as much as they raise their game to levels others can only dream of attaining. From time to time they do put in truly world-class performances, with a test series triumph in New Zealand in 1996 an obvious example of this ability. Then again, they conceded 50 points and lost a series 2–0 to South Africa on home soil in 1997, sending everyone in France into the depths of despair.

The reaction to that was a culling of their senior players and a new-look team that proved to be an inspired choice as we found out at Stade de France. The real problem the French face is that they have so many talented players, they find it almost impossible to get the national team selection right. It's almost as if they have a conveyor belt operating from a rugby-player factory which turns out hundreds of players of real quality each year – ball-handling forwards, pacy wings, backs blessed with that unique gift of knowing where gaps are going to be created in broken play. They have also allowed internal politics to affect national selection to the detriment of international performances.

When they get it right, it's a joy not only to play against the French but to witness the breathtaking beauty of their back play which can be the best in the world. I don't believe any other country can conjure up long-range tries with the flair of the French and, when others try to match this skill, it seems contrived and laboured. Of course, attempting tries from their own line can also be France's undoing but they are prepared to have a go and should be applauded. France are now showing, like South Africa, a greater awareness of what the modern game requires and that is flexibility in approach.

When it comes to World Cups, they have been and are always going to be, a major power. They were beaten by New Zealand in the 1987 final, psyched out of the quarter-finals by England in Paris in 1991, but should have beaten South Africa in the semi-finals of the 1995 tournament. That match was played in terrible conditions in rain-swept Durban and, but for the waterlogged pitch, I believe the French would have made the final again. Perhaps the 1999 World Cup will be their most successful challenge to date. The Southern Hemisphere countries accept that France have the capacity to dominate. The French deserve to be applauded for the work they have undertaken to improve mental and physical discipline. The days have gone when they would implode in the face of English grit and determination and a refusal to be intimidated. Over the last two or three years we have seen controlled aggression in matches with England and it has paid off for them. Being half-Italian, I can empathise with the French when frustration does occasionally creep into their play on the pitch. We play with real passion and that manifests itself in arguments with referees, and in other ways, but it's all part of the commitment we have to the game.

# England

The world's view of the way England play their rugby at test level has changed in recent years and the game has demanded a new outlook. Players are being selected to fit into the way that the coaching panel want England to perform. I have no problem with the way we used to play. If I had been part of the 1991 team or even those sides that were successful in the 1980s, I would have been saying that the results were doing the talking for us. If we had continued in the 1991 World Cup final playing in the way that had got us into the final, I have no doubt the trophy would have stayed in England after the presentation ceremony. We had a great pack of forwards, yet allowed ourselves to be fooled into playing a different kind of rugby and threw the ball around the Twickenham pitch against the Wallabies. You have to play to the strengths of your team and create a situation that allows the individual players to express themselves fully at test level. The pressure is on those individuals because there is no comfort zone or hiding place at the highest level and if you are not prepared to stand up and be counted, another player will take your place. Potentially, this is a very exciting time for the game in England.

I believe that in England we are developing our own style which is unique to us and it has evolved from the character that is contained in the national squad. We are not going to copy anyone else, because our aim is to lead and not to follow, and currently the other Home Union countries don't really know what style they want to play. It's often been said that because England, unlike New Zealand, does not have an agreed style of rugby at club level, we cannot hope to reach our full potential. It is a difficult area to address. Each club is attempting to maximise its success, using whatever talents are available and they may come in the form of players from other Home Union countries. I watched a New Zealand provincial championship game last year in which fourteen of the fifteen Auckland guys were All Blacks. That can only be of benefit to the national team and, as all of the New Zealand provinces play in the same style, it makes it so much easier for John Hart to produce a coherent game plan at international level.

I do see signs that England's top clubs are moving in the right direction, even if it is rather slowly. I put that down to the fact that we are only in our third year of professional rugby in England and in that short period of time there have been significant advances for the game. We are going to have to put our feet on the accelerator because the aim is not to catch up, but to overtake those ahead of us in the battle to be the world's top team. You cannot under-estimate the positive effect that a successful national team can have on the country. England's Euro '96 football win over Holland galvanised everyone. We have to decide, as a country, if we are ready to boost the national cause, or are we content to carry on in the same way and be a mediocre force in the world game. If England and France do commit themselves to the greater national good, they could become unstoppable.

# Scotland, Ireland and Wales

It's no longer enough to issue an annual call to arms and expect Ireland, Wales and Scotland to come up with great performances, because the game is moving on at a frightening pace. Many players from these countries have been attracted to England by the standard of club rugby and the salaries on offer. Various incentives are being tried by national unions to keep the best talent at home, but market forces are taking over. Wales, more than Ireland and Scotland, appears to be able to find the money to retain many of their major talents, but who knows how long that will remain the case? It's a fact that you can no longer, at international level, cover up the holes in your team by relying on sheer nationalistic fervour. You have to be supremely fit, technically efficient and possess the power to compete at the top of the game. Wearing your heart on your sleeve won't bring success if the basic requirements are not present; fervour can only get you so far.

There is immense talent within these three teams and I played with many of those players on the 1997 Lions tour. The point I am making is that, against the very best teams in the world, if there is one player who is not up to the job, he will be cruelly exposed. When Ireland, Scotland and Wales get their very best players on the pitch, they can produce a formidable challenge to any nation. However, you now need thirty players capable of doing a good job for the team, and other countries can afford to leave leading players out and bring in others without any noticeable drop in efficiency or power. This strength in depth is one of the basic requirements for success in the modern game.

I accept that rugby is a sport that does still offer up the shock result, with any drop in mental attitude undermining even the strongest side on paper. But if Wales, Ireland and Scotland continue to play in the way that has brought success in the past, the future of the game will run away from them. They have to try to retain what has been successful and mould that with the new moves that must be made in the game. The danger with this policy is that you get caught between a rock and hard place. Some players can perform in the way that the game now demands but others just cannot attain the standards of fitness and skills that are basic requirements. It sounds harsh, but this is the reality of modern, professional international rugby where you need everyone pulling in the same direction.

# 12
# On tour

## Globe-trotting heaven

I love being on rugby tour and would have revelled in the old-style Lions trips that took you to wonderful destinations for up to six months by ship or plane, involving many stops and new stamps for your passport. I have been to South Africa, Australia, Malaysia, North America, Dubai and all over Europe. But these days, the professional rugby player spends less time in the air, less time socialising and more time trying to beat the opposition on the pitch. Still, the junior club tours keep the old days very much alive and in many ways I envy those thousands of players who head off each year to destinations around the world and remember to play the odd game when they get there! It's a great way of getting to know people because there are periods when you can relax, have a long chat, or reveal hidden talents, be it as a clay-pigeon shot, a singer or even dancer!

Some players blossom on tour while others get homesick. I would be totally at home being a Harlem Globetrotter touring most of the year with some great people in a sporting Heaven. I enjoy the challenges a tour presents, which make you get up and go training in different climates, countries and situations and require, particularly on a long tour, character to come through.

My first sports tour came through football. We visited Germany when I was twelve years old. I was no stranger to travelling in Europe because of my Italian connections, and I thought it was great. At Ampleforth we made a mini-tour to play rugby in London and we also used to travel around the North of England. When I played for Middlesex in the county championship, the four days we spent in Cornwall had all the essentials of a tour because I was able to meet and spend time with players I hardly knew.

## Hanging by my ankles

I felt very lucky to be asked to join Wasps on the senior squad's annual three-match trip to St Jean de Luz because I was one of the young guys at the club, hoping to make an impact and join the first-team squad that season. I hadn't really trained or played with the first-team squad. There were big men and well-known stars at the club and suddenly I was in France sharing a room with six others who could be ten years older than me. There was inevitably a certain amount of let-the-new-boy-do-it boot-room mentality, the highlight of which was when I was held out of a fourth-floor window by the ankles because the rest of the guys in the room decided I was best suited to rescuing the various bits of kit that had fallen off the windowsill, where they had been drying. When you are on tour for only a week and there is a limited amount of kit and the climate is hot, no one can afford to be without their stuff. That's when it became clear to everyone else I was the answer to the problem, and I agreed (God know's why) to be suspended out of the window by Norm Hadley, the 6ft 7ins, 20st Canadian lock. He lowered me upside down so that I could just about reach the kit on a ledge below. Being swung like a pendulum from a fourth-floor window seemed like the best solution at the time! There was another occasion when I woke up and found that one of the lads had used medical tape to tie me into the bed. That produced a real feeling of helplessness but it was all part of the fun of the trip, or so I convinced myself at the time – remember how desperate I was to get into the squad. Off-the-field antics aside, touring also encourages you to grow up as a player and earn the friendship and respect of your team-mates.

## Sending the wrong signals

I was on the Wasps tour to Malaysia where we took part in a ten-a-side tournament. It turned out to be a great example of how to upset the locals by not realising you were causing offence. We got knocked out in the semi-finals which led to a fair bit of socialising in Kuala Lumpar and, for reasons I have yet to discover, some of the lads decided to drop their shorts. We didn't think it had caused much of a stir but the next day we were on the front page of four local papers and the players concerned got arrested and thrown into prison for a day, where they would have languished longer but for the excellent work of the British Consul. What we had overlooked was that we were in a Muslim country where buttocks bared, in however sporting a fashion, are the unacceptable cheeks of English rugby. You have to be aware of these things.

## Lions touring

What touring does give you are fantastic memories that can be shared when you meet up again with people who were on that same trip. The years pass by quickly but the memories last and a special bond develops that is hard for those

Surf's up at Durban; Richard West, Mike Catt, Neil Back and Kyran Bracken auditioning for Baywatch.

*Right:* Doddie Weir dominates another line out.

*Below:* Playing my part in the triumph in South Africa.

who were not part of the tour to understand. Part and parcel of being on new tours is being able to remember what happened last time and the lessons that were learnt.

The Lions tour allowed you time to switch off and relax on your own, which is an important aspect of any trip abroad. When you are in the spotlight, you need to calm things down by letting a bit of air out of the tyre – it can always be pumped up again very quickly. That Lions tour in 1997 gave the players the opportunity to take part in activities they would not normally have tried, including swimming in a cage with sharks floating around nearby. I have to say, my hand stayed down when that particular offer came along, but some of the boys did get up at 5 a.m. to swim with sharks. As I had a five-month-old baby at home at that stage, the idea of voluntarily getting up very early when I could stay in bed and sleep was never going to be an option. However, those who went into the cage thoroughly enjoyed themselves and that is now a great memory from a superb tour.

One of the real delights for me on a tour is to spend time with other players, enjoying their company and talking about everything and anything, even rugby. That's how you get to know people and find out what they are really about because, even in the England squad, we don't spend that much time together during the season.

When a Lions tour comes along there is also the chance to meet the players from the other three Home Union countries who you may otherwise bump into just once a year at the post-match dinner after an international. I was very much in favour of arranging a team meal once a week during the tour because everyone gets fed up at some point with staring at the same hotel walls or doing the same things in the team room that is normally set aside just for the players. We made a habit of doing that in South Africa, no one ever felt left out and the locals dished up some fabulous food.

I have never been on a tour when it got to a point where I said, 'I can't wait for this to be over.' It's always up to the individuals on the trip to make it a success. There is no point in players thinking all that matters is that they are all right; touring is a collective thing and it's up to the senior players to make sure it works. You can tell those players who have been on tour before because they exude a certain confidence and this can help bring youngsters out of their shells and make them believe this really is a great opportunity in their lives, one that should not be missed.

There are bound to be problems on any tour because certain players don't get picked or they are not playing well, or sustain injuries. It's how you respond to these challenges that dictates what kind of tour you will have. It was extremely distressing to have to wave goodbye to someone like Doddie Weir of Scotland, who was kicked off the Lions tour by the boot of a local player. Doddie is a very popular guy and it was hard to find the right words to say in that situation, because he was absolutely gutted. You cannot foresee what will happen on tour and getting injured in sport is a nightmare but one of the occupational hazards we face. Yes, it's very upsetting because you have built your whole life around making a Lions tour and then it is taken away by foul play. You have no option but to try to be positive, be determined to bounce back as quickly as possible, and that is what Doddie did. But that kind of incident makes each player realise how lucky he is and that you must live for each day and make the most of every opportunity a tour gives you.

We will all remember where we were when Jerry Guscott dropped the series-winning goal. Needless to say, I was at the bottom of the ruck and couldn't work out what all the fuss was about! I believe the Lions do have a future and I feel privileged to have been part of the 1997 touring team in South Africa. There is something very special about bringing together players from all four home countries and triumphing against all the odds. The countries that have historically welcomed the Lions on tour would be the first ones to come to the defence of the Lions concept. I know there's no precedent for it in any other sport, but I don't accept it's unfair to use four countries against one nation. Within those four unions you have to get the right balance between different players, so they will pull together in a one-off situation and be capable of taking on one of the great rugby powers. To get people from different cultures, environments and backgrounds to unite under the same banner is an achievement to be treasured and nurtured. It's a fact that the players from the four countries have preconceived ideas about each other and those must be broken down and a new spirit and understanding built in a short period of time. New friendships are forged and each player is able to grow with the experience. The results of past tours show that, when the process is successful, the test matches reflect the harmony and unity and when it hasn't been, the results also reveal that very clearly.

Commercially the 1997 Lions were a great success and it's up to us to ensure that something that was such a massive part of the amateur game is carried into the professional era with care. I didn't really know a lot about the Lions when I was selected, but Ray Cole, a great friend who owns a book store in Fulham, called me when he heard I was picked and kindly gave me a number of books about former Lions tours. It was only after sifting through those pages that it really hit home to me what kind of rugby brotherhood I was entering. You become part of a great rugby heritage and culture and I knew it was a huge honour to be picked.

Growing up, I thought the Lions selectors just picked all the best players from each of the countries and put them in a single team. In effect that is what happens, but there is no guarantee when you go on tour that that scenario will be successful. When you pull on the jersey with the special badge, it doesn't only represent you but also everything that you are made up from at home –

That drop goal; Jerry Guscott wins the test series for the Lions.

*Right:* Not even playing for your country can compare with the experience of playing for the Lions.

your culture and rugby history. That is melted down into the collective which is what the tour becomes. The melding of each team is a unique achievement. Lions tours only come along every four years and by winning selection you become part of a special sporting moment and that must never change.

Getting picked for the Lions was the overriding motivation going into the 1997 Five Nations championship. There was no doubt in my mind that there would be a natural progression from the Five Nations to the selection of the Lions tour party. I started that championship as England's blind side flanker, which was my first aim. We had been pretty poor before Christmas so being picked for the Scots game was a great boost. We beat the Scots well and that did all the England players' chances no harm, we lost to France, and I had to pull out of the Wales game because I wasn't a hundred per cent. I didn't want to undo all the hard work I had put in during the championship so far by taking a gamble and playing badly against Wales. But in the back of your mind is the worry that whoever takes over your test place will have a storming match and then get picked ahead of you for the Lions. England did win but I got picked for the Lions tour. I realised just exactly what I could be embarking on when the initial squad of sixty-odd players assembled and it dawned on me that I had to ensure I was in the final squad because the management made it such an exciting challenge.

I would be prepared to go anywhere at any time to talk in support of the Lions concept. It's a touring tradition that should never be allowed to die. No matter what kind of player you are, you come back a very different person from a Lions tour. You are what you are exposed to in life and the Lions are something unique. Not even playing for your country can compare with the whole experience. When you create a spirit like that it can become almost unstoppable on the pitch. We may not have had the most talented players on the planet in the 1997 tour squad but, ultimately, the sum of the parts was much stronger than the individuals.

# Eskimo Nell and friends

No account of touring would be complete without a few bars of singing. Despite my ancestry, I am not one of the Three Tenors, but I do know the odd rugby song and they still get a good airing, particularly when a team is victorious. We have a short club song at Wasps that is belted out in the dressing room after a win and other clubs have similar homages to past deeds, most lost in the mists of time but no doubt recorded on a charge sheet somewhere in the world! There are some players who appear to have gone to Rugby Song Classes at night school and can reel off endless rhyming tales of debauchery and drink until the bar closes and good luck to them. There was a group of players on the Lions trip who were always ready to sing and that's great because it takes bottle to stand up in front of others and belt out a tune. Singing after a game doesn't mean it has to be a rugby song and many of the Islanders from Western Samoa and Fiji sing hymns or traditional Island songs, accompanying themselves on the guitar. They put on a great show at the various sevens tournaments. Terry Crystal, the England doctor, is always willing to get to his feet on the team coach and lead the boys in a song, and a pianist like my Wasps colleague Damian Hopley is always in demand, while Christian Califano, the French prop, likes to join the band that entertains the teams at the post-match dinner in Paris. Total rugby means that the only time to discover one's team-mates' off-field talents occurs on tour and that is why I love touring.

# 13
# Competitions

## At club level

In England there are three main club competitions: the Allied Dunbar Premiership, the Tetley's Bitter Cup and the Heineken European Cup. Club rugby has been built around the League and Cup and now the European competition has broadened everyone's horizons. You need to finish in the top four of the English first division to qualify for the Heineken Cup, while the Tetley's Cup is open to all clubs in England. There is no doubt that the club fixture list is getting crowded and something has to give – hopefully, it won't be various parts of my body! The League is the primary concern for the clubs as this competition allows them to generate regular support and that boosts profile and revenue. The Tetley's Bitter Cup offers every English club the chance to make a Twickenham appearance and it's a tremendous carrot to dangle in front of even the most experienced player.

In England, we have been too parochial and that is why the arrival of the European Cup has been such a great boost. France possess outstanding talent across a whole range of clubs and we need regular contact. The European Cup also involves the best players from the other Home Unions and this is a competition that can only raise playing standards around Europe. Perhaps the creation of a British league or, eventually, a European super league to rival the Super-12 is the obvious follow on?

The progression from club to international rugby is never easy and the non-playing public does not really understand the giant leap that is required. That's not surprising because only those who have actually experienced this can put it into words. It's often said that your first international goes by in what appears to be a blur. It's amazing how eighty minutes of mental and physical effort pass by so quickly and, suddenly, you are back in the dressing room. In England we have instigated an international fixture schedule that provides players with a series of pre-Christmas matches against the best teams in the Southern Hemisphere. We have to play the best to become the best and I see only positives coming out of this schedule.

# Five (or Six) Nations

After Christmas we have the Five Nations championship which shortly becomes a Six Nations event with the acceptance of Italy, the birthplace of my father. The tournament was first played in the 1880s and that makes it the world's oldest international sporting challenge. Within the Five Nations are a number of old rivalries. The England and Scotland game is still played for the Calcutta Cup which was made from melted down coins belonging to the Calcutta Rugby Club in 1879. The trophy was given a new look by Dean Richards and John Jeffrey who took it for a stroll around Edinburgh after the 1988 match. Afterwards it needed a little help from a silversmith to make the cup look less like a plate! The Five Nations is the jewel in our season and the envy of the rest of the rugby world which is why the Southern Hemisphere countries have created the SANZA Tri-Nations tournament involving South Africa, New Zealand and Australia which formalises an increasing number of test matches between the best teams in the world and makes for compelling viewing. However, I don't envy the All Blacks and Wallabies when they have to fly into Johannesburg and play at altitude straightaway. Stick to Durban and Cape Town, boys. The air is easier to breathe and the beaches make great training areas.

Many people question the timing of the Five Nations, given the problems of bad weather that still exist even now the tournament has been moved out of January. There is a body of opinion that says the end of the season is the best time to play and you could make an argument for that case. But timing these hugely enjoyable competitions to ensure players are in the best possible shape to take part is vital, and staging the Five Nations at the end of a long hard season has obvious drawbacks. However, it would avoid any serious disruptions to the club structure.

# World Cup

The first World Cup was held in 1987, jointly hosted by New Zealand and Australia, and it is already accepted as the greatest leap forward the game has made in a century of rugby. The World Cup gives rugby a stage it previously only dreamt of attaining. I believe the Cup will only get bigger, as long as the organisers recognise that you cannot have the tournament run on buggins' turn. The World Cup is being staged in 1999 by Wales and the other Five Nations countries at a different time of year from when it is hosted in the Southern Hemisphere. Flexibility is needed and it's difficult to see how a rigid set of guidelines can be instigated when the game must be allowed to react to changes, both on and off the pitch. We are talking about a multi-million pound operation, one that generates funds to help keep the game spreading around the globe and no opportunity should be missed to maximise its impact.

The best bid, as happens with other major world sporting events, should win the right to stage the Cup. After the 1987 Cup, the organisers accepted the need to stage the event in just one country and backed this view by agreeing to hold the 1991 tournament in *five* different countries! The 1995 Cup did end up in one country, South Africa, and what a fantastic job they made of it. Who can forget seeing Nelson Mandela, the South African President, walk out on to the pitch for the final between South Africa and New Zealand, wearing François Pienaar's No. 6 jersey. Pienaar, the Springbok captain, will never forget that moment and it was a situation where sport crossed over into politics for the right rather than the wrong reasons. As an international player who has been lucky enough to lead his country, I cannot think of anything more fulfilling than being able to lift the William Webb Ellis Cup before the eyes of the watching rugby world. Our dream can be reality, but only if we want it enough!

# Hitting the big time

The first time I really noticed I was receiving adulation because of rugby came after England won the 1993 Rugby World Cup Sevens. I was lucky enough to be part of a young and talented England squad, captained by Andy Harriman of Harlequins. That World Cup triumph was shared by the whole country and made an impact because no one had expected us to achieve anything. It really was achieved against all odds and that made it even more satisfying. At that stage of my career I had not played any competitive first-team matches for Wasps and to be thrown into a high-profile event was a giant leap for me to deal with. We went through the tournament without feeling any pressure because of that lack of expectation, but that all changed with our triumph at Murrayfield.

All of a sudden I was inundated with letters and telephone calls, I was thrown into a new life and it gives you a tremendous high. You suddenly realise, 'Yes, I have just won a World Cup,' and the enormity of the achievement really hits home. That gave me an insight into what can happen when you and the team put in a performance that catches the imagination of the public.

Only in England can we differentiate between sevens and fifteen-a-side rugby. We say that a particular player who is quick, has good hands and general footballing ability should be seen as a sevens expert. But players like that are what all branches of the modern game needs.

# Playing sevens

Ampleforth had a history of doing well in schools sevens tournaments and I found a tremendous enjoyment in the open spaces the game provides and being able to run at people in a one-on-one situation with the ball in hand. There is little kicking involved in sevens, the ball must be kept in the hand and, to me, that is the purest form of the game – very natural rugby. There is an incredible pain that has to be endured, not only in the tournament, but in training for the event as well. It's an adrenalin hit which may last only fourteen minutes at a time, but what a fantastic high. Those fourteen minutes force you to perform at a level that completely shatters you, mentally and physically, because you can never do enough work. You must always be running, if you find yourself standing still you are not doing the job properly. In that sense, sevens is a tremendous physical challenge and one that brings the best out of me.

After we won that World Cup at Murrayfield, people used to invite me and other players to tournaments in Argentina, Hong Kong, Dubai, Amsterdam, Malaysia or Sicily. I would ask what the catch was, and they said all I had to do was play in a sevens tournament and win it. What a great way to travel the world and accumulate life experiences, while playing a game that you really enjoy. In rugby terms, it was a huge learning curve because we played against some of the great players in those tournaments, men like David Campese, Waisale Servei and John Timu.

I approached these sevens tournaments with the same attitude every time, it was my opportunity to prove that I was capable of competing at the highest level of the game. There was never any pressure because the other nations were always expected to win. But I was able to go out and express myself and I learnt a huge amout from the New Zealand and Fijian players.

Apart from that, you never know who is watching and this was brought home to me leading into the World Cup Sevens. Dick Best was the England coach at that time and was there when I played for a Lords Taverner seven which drew against the English national seven. Dick Best took training sessions with various clubs, including Wasps, and that was my first contact with him at club level after that Taverners appearance. I think he took a shine to me because I responded positively and enthusiastically to what can only be described as his unique sense of humour. I worked hard for Dick and enjoyed the way he structured the sessions and he decided to take a gamble on me and it came off.

# World Cup Sevens

We assembled in Scotland a week before the World Cup tournament kicked off. The squad was: captain Andy Harriman, Tim Rodber, myself, Damian Hopley, Adedayo Adebayo, Justyn Cassell, Chris Sheasby, Nick Beal, Matt Dawson, and

Dave Scully, with Les Cusworth as coach and Peter Rossborough, the manager. All the teams stayed in the same Edbinburgh hotel and that was a marvellous experience because you would bump into the greatest sevens players in the world as you wandered around the place. The first day we arrived in Scotland was Damian's birthday and we decided to organise a few drinks to break the ice and get to know each other better. I knew Damian from Wasps and Matt from England Schools rugby but the rest of the guys were just names I had come across or opponents I had come up against on the pitch.

Training didn't go very well initially, although it was clear that in Andy we had someone who was immensely quick. Sevens is a game that requires the instincts of each player to come to the surface, so there is only a certain amount of training that can be undertaken. You work on defensive patterns and set moves but it comes down to the ability of each player to beat an opponent or create the space to launch a try-scoring move. There is no guarantee that if you pick your best seven players, they will blend into a unit that can be successful. After that Monday night out to celebrate Damian's birthday, we were a little off-beat at training the next day and we had arranged for a Scottish districts side to play us in three matches at 9 a.m. It was deeply worrying that this group of local players beat the national England team in all three matches! We were about to enter a World Cup event that was just five days away with a squad that couldn't even take care of the locals. The management team said to Andy that they didn't know what I was doing in the squad because, on the evidence of Tuesday's training débâcle, they didn't rate me as a player. They wanted to know who had picked this guy because they weren't involved in the selection process. Andy had a quiet word with Les and Peter and explained what had happened the previous night and they realised the players had only slept for a couple of hours – the joys of the amateur days!

I firmly believe that the team bonding on Monday was the most important time we spent together in the build-up to the tournament; we came together as a unit and really created a sense of camaraderie and a desire to achieve something. Of course, no one else gave us a chance because the squad had been thrown together with little preparation and was up against sevens experts like New Zealand and Fiji. But we just got better and better as the week progressed and Andy emerged as the top try-scorer in the World Cup. His pace was a fantastic weapon but there was also defensive work to be done and Andy's try-saving tackle against South Africa won that match and probably enabled us to go on and win the title. He is probably the quickest player I have ever played alongside. Sevens gives you the chance to beat a man one-on-one on a regular basis which just doesn't happen in the fifteen-a-side game, and that is why you can revel in the space offered by sevens. That is exactly what Andy did and he responded with thirteen marvellous tries, including the first in the final against Australia.

*Above:* Dick Best, the former England coach, impressed me with his training drills.

*Left:* The greatest sevens player ever? Waisale Servei of Fiji.

*Bottom left:* What a great sight; Andy Harriman leaves David Campese in his wake in the World Cup Sevens final.

They kicked off and the ball travelled through every pair of English hands before reaching Andy on our own 22 metre line. He was up against the mercurial David Campese. Andy fixed him with a stare and then started running straight at one of the greats of the game. Suddenly Andy used that amazing speed to take Campo on the outside and it was an unforgettable moment as our captain raced downfield to score a critical try. I don't know whose idea it was to name Andy captain, but it was pure inspiration because he played like a man possessed throughout the tournament. As a character, Andy is unique. He has a cavalier approach and never stands on ceremony. We celebrated winning the World Cup in true Andy Harriman style. It was a fairytale finale to a hugely enjoyable week.

I cherish the memory of the shock on peoples' faces when they realised exactly what we had achieved. Geoff Cooke, the England team manager, came into the changing room and congratulated us and the Rugby Football Union put the picture of our World Cup-winning celebration on the front of their handbook, despite the fact that England did not then recognise the development potential of sevens and still don't.

We were quick to reap the commercial benefits of a World Cup Sevens win and yet we did not defend the title four years later with real commitment. I was due to captain the squad in 1997 but Alice was about to give birth to Ella so I was unable to go. When we won the Cup in Scotland, the conditions had suited England with rain and a poorly organised event, featuring early kick offs and long arduous days. Whoever won the 1993 tournament had to be supremely fit to play so many games in just three days. Had the Cup been played in the heat of Hong Kong or the Southern Hemisphere, it may not have favoured England. Four years on, it was clear that professionalism had swept the game world wide and, if we were to defend the Cup properly, the right preparation would be absolutely vital. What upset me was that we had the players and resources to have mounted a successful defence, we could win it again in the future, but you cannot achieve anything without the right preparation in the modern game. We got away with it in 1993 because we caught everyone by surprise and a lot of factors were in our favour. To have repeated that triumph in 1997 in the professional era would have been asking too much under the current structure.

# Wasting potential

The great tragedy about that World Cup-winning sevens side was that Andy Harriman and Tim Rodber were the only capped players in the squad at that time. It took the best part of four years for the national selectors to cap another five members of the squad and that was a long wait. Surely, by winning the Cup we had sent out a positive message, making it clear the sevens squad had something special to offer? After all, we had beaten the world's best. Yet, it took ages for the players to filter through and that's a reflection on how poor the structure used to be. I just don't believe we had people involved at the highest level who had the foresight and courage to take a chance with that group of players. It disappoints me that we continue to downgrade the sevens side of the game.

# 14
# Bar talk

## Should the game have gone professional?

Rugby union had reached a point in 1995 when the rest of the leading countries had moved faster towards professionalism than England. I am not laying the blame for that at anyone's door, it's just a fact of rugby life. In New Zealand the game is the national sport and it was widely held that, in effect, it had been professional for the last ten years. The Southern Hemisphere players were already professional and now we had to catch up. Suddenly it felt to us as if the game was no longer being played on a level playing field. This is because it takes time for professionalism to be fully assimilated and we are going through the process at the moment. It's no mystery why the three major countries, Australia, New Zealand and South Africa, have won the World Cup. No country from the Northern Hemisphere has been good enough so far and that is a situation we are trying to address. Professionalism is still embryonic in English rugby in terms of how the players understand it and how it is perceived by the general public. There is no doubt that other countries have a head start and that must be taken on board.

I admit the game is bound to have lost something by going pro. Those who played in the amateur era, and I include myself, were as dedicated on the field and just as determined to win, all without being paid. But we have to be professional now if we are to win on the world stage and we have to learn the demands of a whole new ball game.

## Will top players suffer burn-out?

I don't believe that, by becoming professional, players are somehow shortening their careers. In many ways the new game can help prolong a career because the players now have tremendous back-up off the pitch in terms of medical help and advice on how best to arrange their eating and drinking habits. In the amateur days, you had a job and that was the way you earned a living, with rugby a demanding pastime. But the top players were only amateur in name and status. When I first came into the game I saw men like Dean Richards, Rob Andrew and Brian Moore dedicating themselves to the game in the same way that any professional would, even though they also had jobs. Now we have the job title to go with the commitment that was always there as an amateur, and you no longer the need to juggle a career and rugby.

My only real concern is the number of matches that we are being asked to play to keep generating gate-takings. That is what is putting the real pressure on the leading players. You cannot possibly play as many games of rugby as football in a season. Rugby is an intensely physical sport which wasn't designed to be played day in, day out by the same player. I don't believe there are more injuries in the game because it is professional and the statistics support this. However, there is a danger that too many matches will create shorter playing careers but, given the right length of season, I don't see burn-out becoming a real issue for the game.

# Are the players paid too much?

The way rugby union went professional was unique in world sport. It all started with rumours of boot money being paid to leading stars in the 1970s. Then we saw in the 1980s the success of the England team opening up the opportunity for players to cash in on their higher profile and earn decent money off the field. When the game went open England jumped straight in to try and get a head start on the other Home Unions. I could see what the birth of the pro game meant at Wasps when Rob Andrew accepted a lucrative contract to become Newcastle's director of rugby. That was the first high-profile transfer. If you believe the rumours, he was offered £150,000 a year for five years which set a precedent for all those who followed him down the same road.

Professional rugby and professional football are still light years apart. Top footballers earn in a week what the majority of professional rugby players take home in a year. Our sport is trying to broaden its spectator appeal but at club level in England we are attracting only 5,000–6,000 fans, when the major football clubs pull in 40,000 a game. In the short term, rugby clubs have had to pay considerably more than they would have wanted to secure the top players – particularly those who are England qualified. There isn't depth of talent in certain positions in England, due to a failure to nurture the grass roots of the game. But as a consequence, because there are only a small number of leading players, the prices they can command are higher. There are players being paid, in the short term, more than they were ever expecting to be offered.

Director of operations, but still in the thick of it – Newcastle chief Rob Andrew.

The mass appeal of rugby has yet to be developed although I am certain it will be created and, in the meantime, other ways of funding the players' salaries have to be found. Things are improving in rugby but much more slowly than in football and the success of the England rugby team at test level is absolutely crucial to the game's well-being as a whole. I don't believe rugby players are over-paid. It's a case of market forces dictating the current levels at these very early stages of professionalism. Some clubs have had to pay large sums to secure the services of players but there is now a plateau being reached as the true ramifications of professionalism are coming home to everyone.

## Should there be a transfer system?

Players are put on the transfer list because there are always winners and losers in a professional sport. It doesn't operate in any shape or form like the football system but rugby is trying to instigate its own market. Players can find themselves surplus to requirements, or they can request a move from a club to further their professional careers. I know people worry that club loyalty will be badly affected by a transfer system, but it's your own playing performances that will dictate where you play and for how long. A player needs to be in charge of his own destiny. If you are performing well and the current club cannot offer you a satisfactory deal, you can move on. If your performance level drops, you start to lose control of your future. These days you are judged more harshly on performance than at any time in the past. Before the game went professional, you could be told you weren't good enough for the firsts and be dropped to the seconds or even further down the playing scale. There was little movement between clubs, unless a player felt he was being badly treated. If a player is being paid a lot of money, he has to justify his position to the public and the club's backers and that makes it a lot more interesting for everyone concerned.

## Are we creating basketball rugby?

There is no doubt that the type of rugby produced by the Southern Hemisphere countries in the Super-12 tournament is a fantastic advert for the game around the world. Players and referees are committed to creating a tasty product for television, which pays a huge sum of money to fund the competition. However, we have to be absolutely clear about why the game is heading down a particular road. Are we changing the rules to satisfy television or to enhance the game?

It's a difficult question because television is the major supplier of cash for the game world wide and their financial resources are vital if the sport is to remain a viable career for thousands of players. The public want to be entertained and I am a great supporter of the kind of rugby we have seen from New Zealand in recent years. It is a heady combination of pace and power, allied to real ambition. In Britain, we are moving along the same road, trying to catch up with the All Blacks before the next World Cup. I believe it is possible to find a balance between the crucial basic elements of the game such as scrum, line out, maul, ruck and kicking, and also to allow the runners to produce the tries that make the television highlights.

A bigger version of sevens rugby with the set pieces reduced to mere restart points would be a mistake and destroy the game's appeal as a sport for all shapes and sizes. Without the need for authentic scrummaging and line-out work, the forwards could all be 6ft 4ins and 17st. They would be designed for eighty minutes of running about the pitch, putting in big tackles. I believe the crowds love to see a 5ft10ins, 18st prop charging down field with a 5ft 9ins, 12st outside half in his way. We are stronger because of our differences and that must never be lost in the search for the perfect game.

# Should referees become professional?

I believe that referees, certainly those at the highest level, need to become fully professional to deal with the massive strides the game is making. They have a very difficult job and it is getting even harder with the rules changing so quickly and the whole profile of the sport rising, increasing the pressure on officials. Despite all the criticism that referees get, there are good officials and some of them are already full professionals. Colin Hawke and Paddy O'Brien of New Zealand and Ed Morrison of England are all good full-time refs. If an official doesn't want to be professional, that's his choice but he should be given the option and they deserve more guidance than they get from the governing bodies. More television coverage means the referee's performance is under more scrutiny than it ever was in the past. Like the players, they are being judged on performance in the new professional age. They do a good job and I don't envy them the problems they face.

I have always been a big fan of the rugby league-style third umpire who rules on whether a try has been scored in the in-goal area. We are talking about crucial decisions and there's no reason why that system cannot be implemented in rugby union. I would also like to see a neutral time-keeper who could take this task off the referee. The man with the whistle has enough on his plate without having to deal with the extra pressure of being pestered by players asking him how many minutes play are left.

# Does rugby involve cricket-style sledging?

There are teams who identify key players in the opposition who they know can be ruffled and plan to use whatever edge can be created. If that involves plenty of verbals, so be it. Mental and physical intimidation is part of the game and everyone knows what's going on. But in many cases the target has been around for a long time and isn't going to be affected anyway. Someone like Michael Lynagh had heard it all before and you were wasting your breath because he just got on with his game. Andrew Mehrtens of New Zealand is much younger than Lynagh, yet he is totally calm in the maelstrom of international rugby. He is very focused and doesn't react to anything you say or do. There are others in the game who can be wound up very easily and if that wins you a penalty or any kind of advantage, that's part and parcel of professionalism. But it's the players who concentrate on the rugby rather than making personal points against an opponent who are the ones who normally end up on the winning side. If you get caught up in a some kind of personal vendetta you let the rest

Mr Cool – New Zealand's Andrew Mehrtens.

of your side down, because where is the ball when you are mucking about? Remaining patient and sticking to the pattern of play, even when you don't have the ball, is vital and no one wants to be responsible for giving away penalties and possibly costing your side the game.

# What do the front rows say to each other?

Now this is a family book and I am not going to give a graphic account of life with that strange breed of rugby player, the front-row forward. If you have ever been caught in a corner by a group of front-row heavies and had to listen to their endless discussions of binding, pushing, pulling and general messing about, you will know what I am talking about. There is a lot of kidology in the front row and noboby misses an opportunity to take a verbal swipe at their opposite number – or a physical one, come to that. There's humour involved – well, what they think is side-splitting – and someone like Jason Leonard is a genuinely funny character, particularly when he's not talking about propping.

Bobby Windsor, the legendary Welsh hooker, was another joker and delighted the 1974 Lions team by coming up with a great excuse for a massive telephone bill while the squad were on tour in South Africa. The team manager was fuming that the bill had been left unpaid as they tried to leave a hotel and he boarded the team bus to find the guilty party. When his first request for the caller to reveal himself was ignored, he shouted out the number which had a Pontypool code – Windsor's home town. With everyone looking at the Welsh hooker, he quickly rose to his feet and yelled, 'All right, I want to know which of you has been calling my wife!'

There are also stories that sum up the front-row psyche but I will refrain from using names to save the innocent and my own skin when I am next at the bottom of a ruck against a particular England player. There was a recent club match where a leading English side took on a touring New Zealand province that included a prop with a legendary bad temper. Up against him on a wet Tuesday night was a current international with a bad back and before taking the pitch the said test star told his mouthy hooker – also an international – not to wind up the Kiwi prop. His back was sore after playing in a Saturday test and the last thing he needed was a great big hairy Kiwi bending him into seven kinds of hell. The hooker nodded his agreement. At the first scrum the packs came together in a mighty crunch and the hooker shouted into the face of the said Kiwi hard man, 'Hey, I've got you on toast. I'm in an armchair and having a great time.' It took the Kiwi some seconds to work out what the hell 'I've got you on toast' meant but, once he realised the mickey was being taken, he proceeded to make life absolute hell for the injured prop. The hooker kept up his verbal tirade all match and the poor English prop sat out the next month's rugby trying to repair the damage, mainly inflicted because of his mouthy hooker.

Other front-row forwards revert to the punch, head butt or knee to make a salient point, but that's probably a sad indictment of their conversational skills, rather than any indication that they are all half-bonkers and mad for a bit of biff.

# Who are the noisiest team you have played against?

That would have to be the All Blacks who are outstanding when it comes to organising their defence which requires plenty of communication skills. Their talk is ninety-nine per cent positive and involves making sure everyone is aware of their duties. Verbal support plays a big part in their play. The All Blacks are past masters at adapting if something is not working in their game plan and to adapt you need to communicate decisions and think on your feet.

The players who make up the spine of your team – hooker, No. 8, scrum half and outside half, plus the open side flanker who organises the defence – are the key decision-makers and need to be heard throughout a match. A scrum half tends to be a player with a good pair of lungs because he is the link between the forwards and backs. A defence that is talking is a defence that is very focused, and that sends out a message to the opposition. It's something I became even more aware of during the Lions tour to South Africa. The rugby league guys in our squad, Scott Gibbs and Alan Tait, made it clear how vocal a team needs to be in attack and defence. They constantly let you know who they are going to tackle and where the ball is heading and I took that on board.

But the game caters for players who like the sound of their own voice and others who hardly say anything. Tom Smith, the Scotland and Lions prop, was the silent man of the tour but, when you get to know him, you enjoy what he has to say. It's just that he doesn't say an awful lot and there's nothing wrong with that. Tom only says things when they need to be aired and many people would say that is a bonus because he doesn't waste energy. That's the beauty of rugby, it's not just the skill and technique you bring to the sport, it's also you as a person and that's reflected in the way that you play.

There are those in the game who don't make a song and dance and do a lot of great unseen work and they are the people I admire most. Wasps is a club that has produced a number of those individuals like David Pegler, Mark Rigby and Dean Ryan and I am sure I have been influenced by how they acted on the pitch. It's had an effect, but a positive one, I hasten to add.

# Should captains chat up the ref?

As team captain there is an obvious need to talk to the referee at appropriate times. There have been many captains who like chatting to the ref during a match. Jon Hall of Bath was always talking away and the same goes for Wasps and Newcastle's Rob Andrew, New Zealand's Sean Fitzpatrick, Dean Richards at Leicester and Andy Robinson, also of Bath. The list goes on and on. We are not being disrespectful to the referee, as they often appear to be in football, and as long as it's a positive dialogue from the captain, it can help the match flow. The days when you had to call him sir are long gone, it's not a public school game any more. Ed Morrison is one of the top English refs who has a good rapport with players all over the world and is a popular export to the Southern Hemisphere for test matches. He is widely regarded as the leading Northern Hemisphere official and he would not be impressed if I went on the pitch and started calling him sir.

Some players do turn to refereeing at the end of their careers, or if injury forces an early retirement, but it's not the first thing that springs to mind when I look ahead to hanging up my boots. I have tried refereeing at schools level and it's a tremendously difficult job. I admire what they achieve in what has become an increasingly fast game.

Mark Rigby enjoyed positive dialogues with the referee.

Jon Hall was another who liked a natter with the ref.

Sean Fitzpatrick works his magic on the referee.

# What about the sin-bin?

I am convinced that bringing a sin-bin into operation would be a great step forward in dealing with foul play and persistent offenders. You have to work out very clearly which offences would warrant a spell in the sin-bin and which would not. There are so many offences you can commit in rugby that it is often difficult to decide which justify ten minutes in the sin-bin, or a penalty, or a sending off. Rugby players are cute and they very quickly learn to play the referee. In other words, they will do whatever they are allowed to get away with. The sin-bin would certainly change the mind-set of players. The period immediately after a player is tackled remains a major problem area for Northern Hemisphere rugby and until this particular aspect is sorted out the game will never move forward at the speed and intensity necessary to rival the Southern Hemisphere. I would certainly advocate the sin-bin to deal with the infringement after a player is tackled. The tackler should be given two to three seconds to roll away before he becomes fair game to be rucked out of the way. Any tackler not making an effort to roll away should be sin-binned immediately. Too often we see the tackled player being penalised. Until we get two teams trying to be positive, the game will not move forward. Referees may need to sin-bin regularly until, eventually, the message will get across!

# Is the points-scoring system correct?

The value of the try has changed over the years and it is currently worth 5 points. I believe we have got it just about right and, with a conversion, the try is worth 7 points, compared with 3 points for a penalty or drop goal. You could argue that the try should go back to being worth 4 points, but the penalty would then have to drop to 1 or 2. The 3-point penalty is still a very valuable commodity, although I recognise the fact that defending teams have the option of committing an offence on the basis that it's better to give the opposition 3 points rather than a possible 7.

The system is logical at the moment as long as referees are strong when it comes to persistent infringement near the try line. You need to act to stop teams deliberately committing offences to deny the attacking team the chance to score a try. It's frustrating for the attacking side and the crowd when a negative team succeeds in stopping a positive one.

The laws of the game are very technical and gamesmanship can come into play when you are dealing with the penalty-try award. Sides can go looking for a penalty try, just as footballers go looking for a penalty by falling over in the box. We don't want that to become a feature of professional rugby and it's encouraging to see football referees penalising those players who try and con a penalty out of the official with a dramatic dive. We have to battle to keep everyone honest or the sport will suffer.

# Do players get a say in formulating the laws?

Most of the current law changes appear to be emanating from the Southern Hemisphere and it's about time England got their act together and started proposing changes that benefit our game. At the moment we are having to follow the lead of the Southern Unions and that puts them at a distinct advantage. For instance, we suddenly discovered that twenty-two players are now allowed to be part of a match squad as the replacements have increased to seven. That ruling came from down under and we had to react. I cannot remember the last time England put forward a suggestion that led to a law change and we, as a country, must seek a more active role. We cannot go on playing second fiddle.

Players are not consulted on the performance of referees in international and domestic rugby and I believe the criteria for picking the best officials forces them to act in a certain way to please the assessors in the stands. That's not a criticism of referees, but if we changed that system we could improve the game. The whole process and structure for officials need to be thoroughly reviewed.

# How much protection are you allowed to wear?

Besides the standard jersey, shorts, socks and boots, players are, under the game's laws, allowed to protect their bodies in certain ways. We can wear a mouth-guard (I never play without one as I love chewing my food with my own teeth!), shin-guards, particularly favoured by the forwards, and soft pads of sponge rubber or cotton wool attached mainly to your shoulders by adhesive tape. It is becoming more common to see players in scrum caps, a feature of rugby in the old days which went out of favour. The old caps used to be made of leather and tied around the chin with laces but the modern version is made of a soft lightweight material with Velcro to keep it on. You can even wear mittens on cold days and the nancy boys on the wing can be seen in these between the months of September and April because, they claim, the forwards don't give them the ball.

Amongst the many things we are not allowed to wear are padded under-garments, gloves and, of course, buckles or rings. There are also regulations about the length and type of studs that can be worn in your boots and recent changes to stud design mean that rubber-ridged soles are accepted as standard. The referee comes into the dressing room before every match to check the players' kit and he can order you to change if he is unhappy with anything. I have seen players ordered to remove excess padding from under their jerseys and that is right. You do not want players trying to emulate American footballers with all kinds of padding and protection. There is a sensible balance that can be achieved and the players and law-makers need to discuss this ever-changing area of the game. Sometimes I do feel a bit like Robocop after the medical team have strapped me up for a match but that is only to help protect certain areas that are starting to show wear and tear during a long season.

## Do we need the Varsity match?

I didn't go to either Oxford or Cambridge and so my view on the outcome of this match is neutral. It has a tremendous tradition and I know that for those thirty players who run out at Twickenham it is a very special occasion, one that remains in their memory for ever. Even before the game went professional, the universities required their squad players to be totally committed to the build-up to the December match and that removes them from club rugby. A player can be tied to a club from an early age these days and by the time he reaches university age, there could be a serious conflict of interests. Logistically, it is very difficult.

Damian Hopley, a member of the Wasps squad, went to Cambridge to win a Blue and when he returned, found he had lost his place in the first team. The standard of rugby Damian had been playing with the club was far higher than at university and he had to battle to get back that place.

The Varsity match sells 75,000 tickets every year which means that a lot of people believe it has a past, present and a future. You could argue that even in the professional era not every good player gets spotted and the Varsity match is a great opportunity for an aspiring player to grab the attention of the top clubs. That has been the case in years gone by and Wasps benefited with a group of very good players from Cambridge that included Huw Davies, Rob Andrew and Mark Bailey. I don't think the match should be abolished but its importance for the national team has diminished.

## What will happen to the Barbarians?

I have only played in one game for the Baabaas, but once was enough to get me hooked. Again, like the Lions, you are talking about a special club and many famous players have been members. The idea behind the club has had an enormous impact within world rugby, but there's no doubt that this is diminishing in the professional era. It's sad that fixtures that used to be held in high esteem have been affected by the changing face of the sport, that Leicester, for instance, have had to cancel their annual Boxing Day game.

I believe that the Baabaas concept must evolve, along with the whole professional game, but there is no reason for it to stop featuring in the schedule. We are now in the era of club contracts and obligations that have to be met on both sides and, when you put pen to paper, you give over your rights to make individual decisions about who you turn out for in big matches. In the old days you had the freedom to choose but that's not the case at the highest level these days; sad, but true.

# Is the new Twickenham stadium a concrete mistake?

I went to the old Twickenham stadium as a mini-rugby player for Kings House, my prep school in Richmond, in 1985. To a thirteen-year-old on the pitch it looked vast and the stands were really close to the field of play. I also went to international games and John Player Cup finals and soaked up the very special atmosphere. I played for England Colts and stood on the West Terrace as England won the Grand Slam in 1991 with the noisy crowd creating a real intensity. I was so close, I felt as if I could have thrown the ball into the line out! The new stadium has lost some of that atmosphere because it goes upwards and back, coming around in a bowl. Those people at the very top of the new stands are a long way from the action and much of the noise is lost by the very nature of stadium's design. It is still a special ground and an incredible place to play your rugby. It's our home, but I believe it is beaten by other grounds in terms of creating a special atmosphere.

If I had to choose my top three, and I would qualify the choices by saying I haven't experienced New Zealand and missed out on the old Cardiff stadium before they pulled it down, my favourites would be Kings Park in Durban, Newlands in Cape Town and the new Murrayfield. It's easy to choose those two magnificent South African stadia because I have fantastic memories of winning there for the Lions in 1997 but that's only part of the reason. They both create amazing atmospheres and the same can be said of Murrayfield where the sound comes tumbling down the stands. I think the new Stade de France in Paris is a very good new stadium, even if the grass had to be spray-painted green! Parc des Princes was a wonderful arena and everyone enjoyed playing there. The new stadium goes back and around but, unlike at Twickenham, the sound is retained much better and everyone feels close to the action which is important. The Twickenham ground was built before the Taylor Report into ground safety was published and they had to try and work out what would be required. The track around the ground means the fans are further away than they used to be.

If I could change anything at Twickenham, it would be the playing surface because we now have the technology to make the pitch even better. I play my club rugby at Loftus Road and that is a superb pitch which helps create the right kind of spectacle. Twickenham is not utilising the turf technology available today and we should be ensuring the pitch is as good as it can get for big games. We need to sow different grass and cut it much lower if we want to boast the best playing surface in the world. I would also change the colour of the seats from boring barbour green to help create a modern vibrant look for the new stadium and the sport.

I welcome the introduction of music before, during and after the game to help maintain the atmosphere and it was great to hear the crowd's response during the half-time break against New Zealand at Twickenham in 1997. There is a balance to be found between retaining the old atmosphere and introducing new ideas that maybe cater for a different type of fan. We cannot afford to become complacent and expect the fans to fill Twickenham just because they always have. We have a duty to entertain off the pitch as well as on it. Fans should want to come back time after time (if they can get tickets!) and the catering and other facilities must be as up to date as possible. We are attempting to do that in club rugby and Twickenham should be the ultimate example of rugby's professional future. There's no doubt that, with a few key changes, Twickenham could become even better. It is still one of my favourite stadia but it has the potential to be even higher on my list.

# Is rugby league on its last legs?

I am a great fan of rugby league and the current England union squad is being helped by Phil Larder, the former Great Britain rugby league coach. We have been able to learn a lot from studying the league game, particularly their defensive play. I believe that both games, league and union, can co-exist without the need for amalgamation. Union has the opportunity to stand right out there on the global stage but it doesn't mean that league will wither in comparison. The league game is restricted to a particular region of England and cuts its cloth accordingly and that is a lesson union has to recognise. The RFU's plan for a regional spread of talent is understandable because you must maximise the game's impact at home as well as abroad. In league, Wigan have dominated the game for a number of years and that has not helped the sport develop because there hasn't been a competitive environment that is marketable. Since the conception of the Super League, things have become much more competitive. Having said that, it still has enormous appeal amongst the faithful.

Rugby union used to lose a host of great players to paid ranks before we went professional. Wales was particularly hard hit by defections and it appeared there was no way back for all that talent. With the decision to go professional, the union game has been able to welcome back those who have enjoyed their time in league but now want to return to the game that first fired their love of rugby. The 1997 Lions benefited from the league experience of men like Allan Bateman, Scott Gibbs, Scott Quinnell, John Bentley and Alan Tait, amongst others, because they were already operating under the kind of fitness and playing regimes the rest of us were quickly trying to adopt. Rugby league is a tough game and that's why I have always admired those who play it. It's a hard way to earn a living, but the sport features a host of natural footballers and the rules help make a fast game that is simple for the fans to understand.

It would be an enjoyable game to play and that is an option I was given during the early part of my career. No one has ever made me a serious offer but a scout from Leeds RFLC came down to watch me and Damian Hopley, my Wasps and England colleague, playing in a League game against West Hartlepool. We lost and both Damian and I played badly which put them off for a while. When Brian Smith went to coach Bradford Northern, as they then were, he showed some interest, and enquired whether I would go professional in 1994–95. I listened seriously to what I was being told but we never got to the point where finance came into the conversation. The whole idea was interesting and that was the closest I ever came to joining a rugby league club.

When Wasps signed Inga Tuigamala from Wigan, the reality of crossing codes struck home. I learnt an awful lot from Inga because he had, basically, been a professional in New Zealand as a union player before he moved to league. He was an example to everyone at Wasps of how to train properly, look after your body and make sure even the small things were done correctly. You had to respect yourself and your team-mates and this code of conduct was something that came through on the Lions tours.

Those ex-league players, as I have already mentioned, were amazingly vocal on the training pitch, communicating in both attack and defence and emphasising the positives all the time. That was crucial to the success of our defensive patterns in winning the test series against South Africa. The training sessions became very lively, vocal and interesting. It was clear to see that they were used to treating rugby as a job – far more than we were at that time.

The change to professionalism in rugby union and the subsequent return of those players who had gone North has opened up the possibility of a union guy going the other way to play the league game without being castigated. It's a game that's played with power and pace, I admire the ball-handling skills and I would consider playing league in the future. Despite the arrival of professionalism, you couldn't say that every union player is comfortable with the ball in his hands in open play, but in league you would never get in the team in the first place unless you could run and pass under pressure.

Alan Tait – back from rugby league and a major force for the Lions.

*Below:* Allan Bateman brought a thoroughly professional outlook to everything he did.

*Facing page:*

*Top:* The irrepressible John Bentley was the heart and soul of the Lions.

*Bottom:* Inga Tuigamala shows that he can pass as well as carry all before him.

# Women's rugby, gimmick or genuine article?

I play for a club that has been at the forefront of the successful expansion of women's rugby in this country and, having coached a lot of young girls and boys at schools in London, I know that both sexes have an aptitude for passing and catching the ball. In fact, the girls at an early age seem to be better at picking up the basics and they listen more intently than the boys, which is not something new! It's enjoyable for boys and girls to play against each other up to an agreed age, but I don't believe that the physical nature of the game will allow the women's game to reach the same level of intensity as the men's version. That is an honest assessment and in no way denigrates those who play women's rugby because their skill levels can be just as high as men's. But you cannot get away from the fact that there is something almost tribal about the muscular contest that cannot be matched in the women's game. However, I am happy to help the women's game in any way I can because England are the former World Champions, so who am I to say they cannot play!

# Should all England matches be played at Twickenham?

One of the shortcomings of rugby league is their need to bring matches to Wembley in order to boost finances by getting a big gate but that means playing away from the heartland of the sport. We need to make sure that, unlike league, union is geographically evenly spread across the country. I accept there is a financial obligation to maximise income in a professional game but the sport must spread its wings. The RFU at Twickenham is the ideal place for our major games and you can argue why build such a major venue if you don't play all your games there. But when you see the success of moving the odd game away from Twickenham to Old Trafford or St James' Park, you must pause to consider the real benefit which such occasions create. A lot of the fans who come to those stadia cannot normally get tickets for Twickenham because the system needs urgent review. There were people at the Old Trafford game against New Zealand who had never been to a test match before and they brought with them a freshness and enthusiasm that everyone was talking about for days after the game.

The Twickenham ticket system is one that I don't understand. In the past, the Twickenham crowd was made up of people who were affiliated to clubs but that has now changed. England's recent success has helped the game reach a new audience and the allocation of tickets should reflect that fact. You don't want to get into a situation where the black market takes preference over the ordinary supporter.

It's a fact that even the players involved in the game find it very hard to get hold of enough tickets and that probably comes as a big surprise. Your name may be in the match programme but you are entitled to only two or three complimentary tickets with an option to buy a few more. It's not an endless supply and that's particularly hard on a player making his debut, because all his family and friends want to support their man and it just cannot happen. Players do get put under pressure by family and friends and it's so hard to say no. I try to avoid all ticket hassles in the run-up to a match; they are an unnecessary distraction, even if it seems bizarre to my friends that I cannot get them tickets when I not only play for the team but also captain my country! Do you think this happens anywhere else in the world? I doubt it.

Twickenham is beginning to move in line with other stadia in terms of the public address system. At Old Trafford there was a tremendous amount of colour and flag-waving that is normally only associated with football and it made a real impact on me. It was an indication of a different kind of supporter base. If you turn up at Twickenham with a flag, they are likely to ask you to leave it outside. That is the kind of attitude we have to change and make sure that wherever we take the England team and call it home – St James' Park, Villa Park or Old Trafford – it should be a place capable of intimidating the opposition into feeling they are entering an arena. That day at Old Trafford gave me an inkling of what it must be like to be at Manchester United player – heavens, what a thought for a Chelsea fan – because you were so close to the supporters. We appear to be so far removed at Twickenham, whereas the passion of Old Trafford really made an impact and those supporters generated a wall of sound.

It wasn't unusual to have to call the line-out signals four or five times because the noise made it so hard to hear anyone talking on the pitch. That is why we kept on going into a huddle because it allowed us all to understand the call. Although that slowed the game down, it did ensure we knew where the ball was meant to be going. You don't tend to hear individual comments until someone is attempting a penalty kick, like my team-mate Gareth Rees, of Canada. Now Gareth is not the slimmest player in the world and tends to attract cries of 'Your dinner's ready' and 'You won't get this one, fat boy'. But he blocks them out by going into a mental tunnel which means he is only focused on the job in hand as yet another kick sails through the middle of the posts.

I have never felt like crossing over the touch line to remonstrate with a fan. By doing that, you would be admitting that his comments were having the desired effect. If you do get annoyed, you should be questioning your own concentration level. Spectators pay a lot of money to watch any sporting event these days and they are entitled to their opinions, be it 'Come on, Wasps' or

'Come on, fat boy', so you just cannot allow that to affect you. In rugby support can mean a great deal with teams lifted by the roar which tumbles down from the stands and that was a huge factor at Old Trafford.

# Are there too many overseas players in the English leagues?

This is the major argument in the game and it is has been complicated, like so much else, by our entry to the EC. Under European law you cannot restrict the movement of workers, so English rugby clubs are not restricted in the number of French players, for example, they can sign for their first-team squads. However, the RFU allows you to field only two non-EC players in a match squad, though the law can be side-stepped when players from outside Europe find a way of gaining a passport from an EC country.

I have English, Irish and Italian blood. I was born here and feel totally English and that is why I opted to play for England. If I had decided to go for Italy people would have been justified in asking why was I allowed to play my club rugby here if I didn't want to represent England. It's a very difficult question and, given the way the European Community has come together, it is becoming even tougher to find an answer out of court. Players are able to look down their family tree until they find an Irish or English grandparent which gives them the right to play here as non-overseas player. I don't think the regulations are working and I believe that to be eligible for a European qualification you should refer only to the nationalities of your parents; going back to grandparents opens the gates too far. England set up the rules and regulations for our own League and there should be stronger guidelines. A financial incentive for clubs to pick more England-qualified players is one option that has been touted around to deal with the question of overseas stars.

I worry that even more world-class players who get to a certain age and want to cash in on their success will look to England as the League in which they can extend their careers for a couple of years. You cannot blame them. The benefits can be a real bonus for a South African, say, who is getting paid in pounds. He will be earning nine rand to the pound and a couple of years in England will make him a millionaire in his own country.

Some players may want to broaden their horizons and experience a different rugby culture, as Thierry Lacroix did when he left France for South Africa. It's a fact, however, that every province or state in those Southern Hemisphere countries is prepared to concede a little bit in terms of their squad in order to help the national cause by playing a home-grown youngster rather than buying in a star player. I don't think there is much chance of English players heading to South Africa.

Robert Howley – on the way to another try against Wasps.

Philippe Sella and Michael Lynagh (right) were central to Saracens' Cup triumph in 1998.

Some of the Home Unions have incentive payments built into the player contracts in an effort to keep them at home and ward off offers from English clubs. If you are Welsh, you will argue that it's vital that Robert Howley plays scrum half in Wales, while the director of rugby at a top English club would counter that it's important that Howley plays at the highest possible level to help improve his game. For the good of the game globally, it's vital that we don't see talent focused on just one competition in one country. That will create a damaging disparity and recent results in the Five Nations, where one country has hammered another, will be seen more often.

It's important that more countries are able to mount a credible challenge for the World Cup rather than the same five each time the event is staged and that's why countries like Scotland, Canada and Argentina should be brought along and have strong domestic rugby set-ups. You do not want a rugby league type of scenario where Australia wins the World Cup all the time.

If you look overseas to New Zealand, South Africa and Australia, the power-base of the game in the world today, they do not have many players from outside their own countries. The way that those countries finance the game and have built their infrastructure promotes the development of local talent. True the Island nations of the South Pacific supply many players to domestic New Zealand rugby but that comes under the special political arrangement they have in that region. Overall, it's not a rugby area that features many overseas signings because they do not need to import talent.

That isn't the case in England and if there were enough English players with the right talents, we would not have bought in so many foreign stars. Rather than bemoaning the fact that overseas players are in our league system, we should be concentrating our efforts on ways to make it unnecessary in the future. The clubs will always look at the possibility of bringing in overseas players when they cannot generate their own talent. If there was no relegation from the Allied Dunbar premiership, clubs could focus more on performance than results. The fear of failure and financial ruin would be avoided and clubs would be inclined not only to play exciting rugby, but also to push young talented England-qualified players into the team far earlier without the fear factor. This would keep a lid on the need for overseas players.

Having said all that, one has to admit players like François Pienaar, Joel Stransky, Zinzan Brooke, Michael Lynagh, Philippe Sella and Inga Tuigamala are great box office for the game and provide valuable role models for any up-and-coming players. These are icons of the game and have set the standards that everyone else aspires to and they are performing week in, week out, in England. It's a real pleasure to play against someone who you have looked up to in the game but I realise that there are many who want English players filling that particular position in the team.

We spend too much time worrying about the overseas players we have and not enough on how to end the need for their services. How many English people do you see playing Super-12 rugby in New Zealand? None, because they are producing so many home-grown players that regulations are not required and it's that kind of investment in the future that should be the motivating factor for the RFU and the clubs. I accept that it is more difficult in this country because, unlike in New Zealand, rugby is not the number one sport and central to our culture. If you are male or female and fit to play in New Zealand, it's rugby you opt for. We have to try to expand the game here to give ourselves a chance.

In business it is tempting to look at the short term rather than the long term because you are pumping in large sums of money and want reward as soon as possible. Chelsea under Ruud Gullit worked on the same basis as the Ajax football academy and that involved bringing on youngsters who come into the first team equipped to make a real impact and a living from their chosen sport. We, in rugby, are starting to understand the relevance of long-term planning and top teams have their own academy teams, which is very encouraging for the future of the game.

Many people have talked about the lack of English alternatives to the foreign stars and that is true, but not in every club. There are English players who are not reaching the right level because there is a foreign player in their way. In other countries, the national team is the be all and end all of the game, but here we have other factors governing the sport and you cannot ignore the financial question. I do support a limit which governs the number of overseas players in English rugby as long as we commit ourselves to developing our own talent with a clearly worked out plan which involves the whole of the game. We have the largest pool of talent in the world and why should we be the ones who are buying in overseas players? We need to take a long hard look at ourselves.

# Should players go straight into coaching?

This is a decision the individual has to make and it would be inappropriate for me to point a finger at a specific case and say that someone has gone into coaching too early and that becoming a poacher turned gamekeeper is a bad move. When you play the game at the highest level it does get into your blood and many players find it difficult to cut the ties once their playing careers are over. In the past we lost too many great players because they did not feel able or ready to offer their considerable insight and ideas, but that is now changing. With professionalism, there is another career open to former players, and we need their intelligence and skills because, in this country, we are not blessed with a large pool of great coaches who are crying out for jobs.

This is the way we do it in South Africa – François Pienaar offers more sound advice.

In many respects, the players who turn their attention to coaching bring a real understanding of current problems and this goes right across the sporting board with football a prime example of what former players can achieve in management roles. Player-managers are more prevalent and in rugby union we have seen the arrival of player-coaches like François Pienaar at Saracens and Mike Brewer at West Hartlepool, while stars like Dean Richards and Andy Robinson are coaching or managing major English clubs immediately after finishing their playing careers. They feel confident in their ability to do the job and know what's required to win allied to the critically important fact that they actually enjoy what they are doing.

The players will respect someone who has been at the coal face, as long as they can at crucial periods distance themselves from those who were until recently team-mates as well as friends. There comes a time when you cannot be nice to old mates and that cut-off time is often when you discover if the new relationship is going to blossom or become a real problem with clashes of personality. The players have to accept that their former team-mate does have a new role, one that sets him apart from them and they have to respect that position.

## Will the Six Nations championship be a success?

Allowing Italy to join the Five Nations in the 1999–2000 season will ensure that all the competing teams are involved throughout the tournament. It's very frustrating to put in a good performance and then have to sit on the sidelines for a month because it's your turn for a blank fixture. It doesn't matter if you have won or lost, that inactivity is frustrating. Italy warrant inclusion and I am not letting my Italian blood talk here; their results against the other European rugby powers prove they are a dangerous team. Italy have been asking for a place in the tournament for some time and now all the effort has resulted in their acceptance, I am delighted. Italy are at a stage where they can regularly beat teams that in the past would have considered them to be an easy match. Like most things in Northern Hemisphere rugby it seems to take an age to get a decision made and I expected Italy to be admitted earlier. I accept that if the Italian team suffer a few injuries, their strength in depth can be exposed. We put a big score on them while they were short of a few key men. From an English spectator's point of view the thought of an away trip to Rome must be whetting the appetite and, who knows, with the Italian infrastructure and magnificent football stadia, you would not write off their chances of staging a World Cup in the near future. Gastronomically it would be a stunning success and players would not complain about food poisoning at any point in the tournament! It would be something special to stage a World Cup final in the San Siro in front of more than 100,000 fans and if Italy made a bid to stage the event, the IRB would have to consider that application seriously.

Many people have questioned the future of the Five and soon to be Six Nations tournament and I would just like to point out a few facts. Wales were given a sound beating at Twickenham in February 1998 and critics started talking about the demise of the championship and dark days for everyone but England and France. Well, I remember, as a passionate England fan, having to deal with repeated beatings from the Welsh and older friends tell stories of turning up at work to face a Welsh colleague who was only too happy to recount in every detail the play of Gareth Edwards, J.P.R. Williams and Phil Bennett in the most recent win over England in the 1970s. Now, we can say, this is pay-back time for all those wallopings we took. Teams do have difficulties at various times and the real point we should be debating is whether these troughs will become prolonged because of the advent of professional rugby.

The Five Nations is a wonderful tournament but it needs to change with the times and maybe the structure of the matches could be reviewed. In 1998 the two top teams were France and England and the result of that match – the first in the championship – was always going to have a massive bearing on the final positions. It must be possible to work out a different fixture schedule that takes into account the finishing positions of the teams in the previous year's championship. I want to keep spectators and television viewers interested for the entire tournament and this is one way of achieving that aim.

We are also obsessed with the top tier of European rugby and that ignores the likes of Spain and Germany who are improving as international opponents. They should be operating in a competition that runs alongside the Five/Six Nations, which would give a country like Germany a real incentive to continue the dramatic expansion of the game. I understand they started with around twenty clubs and now they have 120 which is an indication of the potential for a sport that they have only just started to embrace across the country. I have no doubt that the Germans would get everything technically right, if nothing else, and have the best scrummage machine in the game! They would also be very good if it came down to a penalty shoot-out in a World Cup match, although this time we would be OK if we kept on kicking the ball over the bar! There is a healthy future for the tournament and who am I to argue about the inclusion of Italy; they offered me the chance to play international rugby before England spotted me.

# 15

# The way ahead

## Physical mayhem

The purists take great delight in watching the moment when two scrums pack down for the first time. I know this is true because I have listened to endless boring discussions between old front-row forwards. The physicality of that battle in the scrums amazes fans and experts alike, while others are delighted by the sight of the ball being moved down the three-quarter line with pace and precision; two people matching each other for speed on the wing and eventually one of them emerging the winner to score. There is the purely physical battle for supremacy, while on another level there is the mental struggle for domination over your opposite number or the opposition team as a whole.

I am totally biased, but rugby is a game that allows spectators to see those competing strain every sinew in what is the closest thing to war in sport. It's tribal and very physical and no one is pretending. It's not illegal and no one is going over the top because there is an acknowledged line that you have to stick to if the game is to flow and be exciting. Anyone who has found themselves at the pitch side for a major match will have been amazed at the hits that players give and take during normal play. It's quite special to behold. You go out to do battle and what interests me is seeing which players clearly are ready for the intense physical challenge and which are patently not.

The environment in which the game is played is very special. You have two sides legally knocking hell out of each other for eighty minutes and then they shake hands and have a drink in the bar. That's the human side of rugby, a carry-over from the amateur days, and it's something we have to fight to retain. I realise that 'jobsworths' and no-go areas in stadia are creeping into the game as result of the professional era. There is a danger that in the modern game a player will turn up, play and then depart.

The higher up you go in the game, as a player and supporter, the greater and more intense the atmosphere becomes. Anyone who was at the England games against New Zealand in 1997 and the World Cup finals, knows you can cut the atmosphere with a knife. At the moment there is a genuine honesty and respect in the game which also exists between the supporters. Even though the fans feel this tremendous passion and loyalty for their team, at the final whistle both teams and sets of supporters congratulate each other and that must not be lost either.

International rugby attracts supporters who are not generally committed to the club game and we have to win them over because you have to accumulate to survive. Bums on seats is, I realise, a rather crude way of discussing the subject but that's what we are all aiming to achieve and the larger the crowd, the happier the financial controller will be at the end of each season.

# Taking and giving

The sport has undergone massive change in the last couple of years and it is still evolving. The process has at times been painful and there is one aspect of rugby that does concern me. To do anything in life you have to be passionate and absolutley determined to be the best. Enjoyment and success go hand in hand and I fear that the sport is starting to attract players who are achieving success without enjoying the game in the same way many still do, win or lose. People always tell me I am a lucky person to be able to play rugby and be paid for doing something I really enjoy. They often wonder what I would have done in other circumstances and I reply that I would do what they are doing – only better! That's because I give a hundred per cent to anything I set my mind to and that is always the case. I don't want to look back with any regrets.

When I first joined Wasps it was in the amateur era and I was in awe of the players who were already there and had achieved international success. There was such a deep-rooted respect for those players and you appreciated they were men who had learnt their trade and were now performing at the highest level. I felt very humble in that environment and knew I had a lot to learn. It was a boot-room culture, one in which you did what you were told and, in return, those experienced old hands passed down their knowledge of the game. I don't believe there is this two-way exchange in the current game and that's worrying, because it will be the ones who have the knowledge who develop quickest. In any professional sport there is a capacity for selfishness and greed and I see a lot of young guys who have all the trappings of success – the mobile phone, club car, branded leisure wear and big salary – and haven't really had to do an awful lot to earn it.

There is a real danger of a lack of respect amongst peers. You play the game to get peer respect and maybe, when those who started under the amateur banner fizzle out, things will change and rugby will become just a ruthless environment. In the time I have been playing, the most important thing is to come off the pitch having earned the respect of the players around you; not just your own team, but also from the opposition, and that's what drives me on to dominate a game. One of the greatest assets you can possess as a player is the ability to listen to those around you and that's something I realised from an early age. OK, you may not agree with everything that is offered, but one thing might make sense and it can be added to your game and be useful throughout your career.

Too many players these days take things for granted and don't realise the opportunity they have been given and the special environment that has been created by the efforts of others to produce professional rugby union in this country. You can't help thinking of that formidable player Brian Moore who managed to combine a career as a successful litigation solicitor with hooking for England, which is amazing. Brian often had boxes of work with him at the team hotel in the week leading up to an international and somehow switched from one to the other. That is a heavy mental task to set yourself and I have the utmost respect for all those players who juggled a career and rugby in the amateur days. You shudder to think what the players of yesteryear, men like Gareth Edwards, Barry John, Mike Gibson and David Duckham, who were amateurs holding down a job and making time in their lives for sport, could have been like in a professional era. Someone might argue that it might have been to their disadvantage, but I disagree. To be given the environment to be the best you can be is a wonderful opportunity. If I have one wish it would be that the young player coming into the game realises the opportunities available to him. Hopefully, it will come and we will have a greater respect culture. Rugby has yet to settle down in the professional era and it is up to those of us who are involved at its inception to ensure the sport grows in the right way.

# Burning the old school tie

Rugby is no longer a game dominated by players who went to particular schools which offered the sport on their timetables. It needs to be a far broader-based game that anyone can play. If you work hard and dedicate yourself to the game, it doesn't matter what school you went to.

In the past, I believe the English game did suffer from the perception that it was a sport played by a minority who went to the right schools. But the success of England in the last ten years has helped people look at the game in a different way. You can now play rugby and not feel in some way inferior to other sports.

Each World Cup has had a positive effect on the growth of the game in this country and that will continue. The 1999 World Cup, being hosted by Wales but jointly staged by the Five Nations, is going to be crucial in terms of generating new converts to the sport.

Brian Moore has his head screwed on after the battle.

Mickey Skinner in all his glory.

Players like Jason Leonard of England have helped break down old prejudices. Jason comes from the Barking area of East London where West Ham dominates the sporting psyche. But it is also home to many successful rugby clubs and he found his way to Barking RFC, despite playing sport at a school that was football orientated. The English Schools selectors cannot afford to restrict themselves to a small number of famous rugby acadamies like Ampleforth, where I was educated. The net is being spread wider than ever because we are now a professional sport, competing for a limited number of talented youngsters.

Clubs have recognised this need to cultivate young talent and many run their own recruiting systems in order to identify potential professional stars when they are barely into their teens. At the same time, the clubs and rugby unions, recognise that it's far from healthy to start imposing professional ethics and training routines on a junior player when he should be enjoying a rounded education. That is why special scholarships are being offered that involve university education and courses designed to allow a player to cultivate the skills needed to communicate and adapt to a changing world. The game would be ignoring its wider responsibilities if it did not equip these young men with the tools that are necessary for a life away from rugby. Players normally retire in their early thirties – injuries allowing – and that leaves an awful lot of time to be used for something other than chasing a rugby ball around a pitch. I followed a course at Kingston University before the game offered me the chance to go full time.

For some players rugby is a way into a media career. We have seen Jeremy Guscott launch a radio and television career as a presenter and Will Carling, his England centre partner for so long, is the front man for ITV's rugby coverage. Paul Ackford and John Taylor, two former Lions forwards, are the rugby correspondents for leading British papers, while Ian Robertson, a Scotland outside half, is BBC Radio's rugby correspondent. Fran Cotton and Steve Smith, two ex-England captains, run a very successful sport clothing company and these are just some of the avenues close to the game that open up for ex-players. Dawie de Villiers, the former South African captain, and Hugo Porta, Argentina's greatest player, have become successful political figures as sports ambassadors although, somehow, I can't imagine walking into an offical function at the British Embassy in Delhi and being greeted by Mickey Skinner, our representative in India, with the cry of 'Ship them in, fat boy!'

# Fostering the future

Community contact is a vital area for clubs and Wasps make sure the players get out into the schools and clubs of the area to spread the rugby gospel, for that is the only way we will ensure English players are ready to take over from overseas stars in the near future. This is the most important investment for the future of the game and we should learn from the successful programmes operating in New Zealand and Australia to target new talent. If there are excellent facilities on your doorstep, why not use them for the benefit of the local community. Clubs must increase their supporter base because rugby is only one of a number of professional sports vying for attention. At the moment, when we visit local schools the children take part in our sessions wearing Arsenal, Chelsea and Manchester United replica shirts. I hope that the time is fast approaching when Wasps and Saracens jerseys are also in evidence. We need to show these youngsters an alternative and make it as attractive as possible. Creating a successful England team is the biggest help to any drive for new players and fans. This game can teach young people skills, give them a career option and even help them learn humility, which is not a bad thing these days. If just one or two of the youngsters grow up to become a Rory Underwood or Rob Andrew, we are doing our job.

## Some final thoughts

I can now look back and reflect on certain occasions in my career, like getting picked for England, then the Lions, and being given the captaincy, with great pride and a real sense of achievement. But I am also looking forward to the rest of my career. I want to be able to say in four or five years' time that I did everything I possibly could to be the best and have no regrets. Being able to come home to Alice and our daughter Ella ensures I maintain a sense of perspective and that is vital for a life outside rugby. I need to spend time with them because a happy life away from the game will help me get the most out of my sporting opportunities.

Different people play the game for different reasons and, from my point of view, it's not for money because I started long before that was a key element. I play rugby for enjoyment and winning, and the chance to earn the respect of my own team, the opposition and the referee. We all want others to respect us as a player and a person but it's not always the case. You can be respected as a person but not as a player and vice versa. I would like to think I can earn respect in both ways through the way I play and act. Many players can pull out a big performance at various points of the season, but the measure of the great players, be they in golf, basketball, cricket, football or rugby, is their ability to perform at a consistently high level week in, week out, regardless of the outside pressure their success attracts. That's the great challenge and the one I am determined to take up.

# My sporting heroes

My father was originally from Parma and moved to Turin during the Second World War. He has always been passionate about football and is still a mad Juventus fan. Whenever we went to Italy I was exposed to this marvellous sporting heritage and, when at home, we went to see Chelsea. It's quite a coincidence that I am a great Chelsea fan and they now have a strong Italian connection. When we moved to London we lived in Barnes and I could have chosen Fulham, Brentford or even Queens Park Rangers, where Wasps now have their home ground. But Dad always had an affinity with Chelsea and from the age of seven or eight I learned to be a Blues fan. At that time they weren't a great team and, although they were in the first division, were not that successful in the League or the FA Cup. Clive Walker was up front, Mickey Droy at the back and Peter Bonetti was finishing as goalkeeper. Although it wasn't a great period in the club's history, when I went it seemed they always won which made the occasion all the more enjoyable.

My early heroes were George Best, Denis Law and Bobby Moore. My first rugby hero was Bill Beaumont. In those days, not having gone to regular matches, I was restricted to seeing internationals on the television. Other England players like David Duckham and Steve Smith also spring to mind.

Setting the No. 7 standard – Peter Winterbottom bursts away.

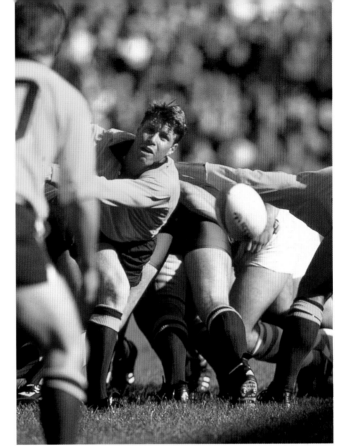

Nick Farr-Jones fires out another superb pass to Michael Lynagh.

*Below:* David Campese – striding out in his inimitable fashion.

Later it was Rob Andrew and the person who could best be described as my childhood hero, Peter Winterbottom, the England flanker.

When I first watched New Zealand, I became aware of this amazing player in their back row with a strange name, Zinzan Brooke. It seemed that there was a set of rules for every player except Zinzan, as he took little regard of the laws and made them up as he went along. He was ahead of his time as a player. He was someone who appeared to be able to do what he wanted on the pitch, rather than what other people told him to do. That was a major difference that attracted me to him because so many players do what they are told. I still look forward to being able to drop a goal in a vital test match like Brooke – and they do go over when I try them in practice, so who knows? Even some of the very best players have an area of weakness, a flaw in the game which may be kept hidden for much of the time. With Brooke, I don't think that is the case, and now his brother Robin is playing very well and has become as complete a player in the second-row position he occupies. For a player like Brooke to win as many caps as he did in the competitive back-row position for a country like New Zealand is quite phenomenal. The Kiwis don't allow their players to remember too many bad games without bringing someone else into the side. Zinzan Brooke is a true rugby warrior and always responded to a challenge.

# The team I would love to play in

We all love to play this dream-team game and the fifteen players listed here are the ones I would get a real kick out of taking the field with for a match played at Super-12 level or above under the current laws. Yes, I could have delved into the past, but just because my team comes from 1987 onwards doesn't mean I don't have a massive regard for all of the great players from the past. I am only too aware of this great game's heritage and men like Gareth Edwards, Jack Kyle, Jeff Butterfield, Ian Kirkpatrick and Jan Ellis are legends to me, too.

I have chosen these players because they could, under the current laws, play the game at a level that would thrill whoever could afford a ticket to get into the chosen ground. So, here we go with my dream team:

    15  Serge Blanco (France)
    14  Jeff Wilson (New Zealand)
    13  Philippe Sella (France)
    12  Jeremy Guscott (England)
    11  David Campese (Australia)
    10  Michael Lynagh (Australia)
     9  Nick Farr-Jones (Australia, captain)

1  Christian Califano (France)
2  Sean Fitzpatrick (New Zealand)
3  Olo Brown (New Zealand)
4  John Eales (Australia)
5  Robin Brooke (New Zealand)
6  Me (of course!)
7  Michael Jones (New Zealand)
8  Zinzan Brooke (New Zealand)

I would appoint Nick Farr-Jones captain following his marvellous career with the Wallabies, culminating in the 1991 World Cup triumph, and his partnership with Michael Lynagh would be worth paying to watch on its own. The pack leader would be Sean Fitzpatrick. That would leave me free of any responsibilities and able to just put my twopennorth in whenever I felt like it – even if it wasn't wanted!

It is a side containing all the elements that I believe are necessary to bring the current game alive on the pitch and I would have a sizeable bet on us against anyone. People may say 'How can you go into any game without Christian Cullen, the New Zealand full back?' But Serge Blanco gets my vote. He was that special and just look at the two wingers who would be working alongside him – David Campese and Jeff Wilson. What a back three, what a side.

You may not agree with my team but that's one of the beauties of this marvellous, unique game that I love. Do your own in the bar, preferably on the back of a Wasps programme.

# Index